The

@rchers
@narchists'

A–Z

The
@rchers
@narchists'
A–Z

Ian Sanderson

B◼XTREE

First published in Great Britain in 1998 by Boxtree
an imprint of Macmillan Publishers Ltd
25 Eccleston Place London SW1W 9NF
and Basingstoke

Associated companies throughout the world

ISBN 0 7522 2442 5

Text design by Blackjacks
Typesetting by SX Composing DTP
Printed and bound by Mackays of Chatham plc

Dedication

This book is dedicated to Simon Pemberton and Clive Horrobin — two giants among men who did their darndest to shake the cosy establishment of Ambridge by respectively creating and reapportioning wealth. To their detractors we would just say, let he who is without sin ...

Disclaimer

There are two things we need to get straight before you get going. First it is impossible to write a book about something that changes and evolves six times a week and expect it to be up to date. By the time you are busily scanning these pages we will probably be accusing Higgs of having verbal diarrhoea, Kate's child will turn out to be an Eskimo and Shula will be slowly drowning in a vat of boiling oil. Nevertheless every word herein was gospel at the time of going to print.

The other thing is that any similarity between persons mentioned in this book and people alive or dead is completely intentional and anyone upset should just lighten up a bit.

Acknowledgements

We would like to thank the BBC for bringing us *The Archers* through all these years and giving such enjoyment to the lives of so many of us. We would not like to thank Mr Boyle, Controller of Radio 4, for changing the start time of every episode, cutting the length of the individual slots and adding an extra one at a time when we don't want to be listening, although we do appreciate at last having an omnibus edition that is unexpurgated. We particularly don't want to thank him for telling us that all his changes were the result of a great amount of 'consultation' as if a load of *Archers* listeners had spontaneously risen up and requested the dog's breakfast we have now. We wouldn't like to thank the BBC for refusing to advertise Archers Anarchists after the programme whilst continuing to advertise Archers Anoraks.

Archers Anarchists

You may be a suitable candidate for joining Archers Anarchists. If you think you can cut the mustard send an A5 stamped addressed envelope to:

Archers Anarchists,
15 Hewgate Court,
Station Road,
Henley-on-Thames,
Oxfordshire RG9 1BS.

Introduction

In 1995, the Archers Anarchists emerged as a movement dedicated to the eradication of castism. For students of the 'ism', castism may be regarded with curiosity, to *Archers* listeners it is an evil with which we have been forced to live for a great many years. It is the only word which suitably describes the tendency of the media to parade photographs purporting to represent characters from Ambridge. Listeners know what the characters look like and the last thing we need is to be assaulted by the images of a load of dreary microphone-bound people claiming to be our friends.

But the Anarchists are much more than a single-issue organization. Shocked by the antics of the dreaded Archers Addicts (an establishment fan club run *for* anoraks *by* anoraks and completely in the pocket of the BBC), it was recognized that an independent rallying point was needed. The dreaded Addicts claim to be 'run by the cast', something which all Anarchists know cannot be anything but a malicious falsehood. The BBC, which is prohibited from advertising on its terrestrial channels, frequently pumps out recruitment pleas for its poodles, and we have to fight from the trenches. Not that we're bitter mind you.

The world is full of people who take the side of the underdog, but you won't find that namby-pamby posturing from Archers Anarchists. No, we stand four-square behind the overdog. As far as we are concerned, underdogs are wimps: people who think the world owes them a living. That's why, when Jailbird snivels, Shula shrieks, The One-eyed Monster moans or That Fisher Woman pontificates in her offensively right-on manner, we would lock 'em all up and use them for testing the effects of state-of-the-art twenty-first-century biological weapons. Here they are Saddam, you only have to ask mate.

You may think Archers Anarchists are nasty, vicious, insensitive, uncaring, mean, and even stupid but we love *The Archers*. Indeed, like millions of people across the land, we devote 65 hours a year to listening.

There are many official publications about *The Archers*, not least of which are a number that purport to describe the characters and institutions. We realized that there was a gaping hole in all these scribblings, namely THE FACTS. Recent listeners will never have known that nice old Uncle Tom is a murderer, whilst those very new to Ambridge life may not realize that we have several other murderers living in the village – Dr Death, The Village Bicycle, Shula Hebden, and her brother Dayveed. *The Archers Anarchists' A–Z* seeks to strip away the gloss and the cosiness of *The Archers* and tell you instead what really happens.

As you are reading this book, always remember this is an anarchic A–Z, so don't expect to find everything here. If there's something or someone you expect to see listed but isn't, then tough. It's either because it was too boring to write about, or because we've forgotten. Fair enough? Be prepared for some revelations and scotching of a lot of cosy myths. The BBC establishment and their mates, the dreaded Archers Addicts, will lead you to believe that it's an 'everyday story of country folk'. Everyday story 'moi oi' as the late Jethro Larkin would have said. It's about serial murder, slaughtered animals, deceit and rampant sex, punctuated with nauseating globs of syrup and ladles of hypocrisy. And we love it. If you can't take it, don't read any further, use the book to prop up a wobbly table leg instead.

Glossary

As you peruse this A–Z you will encounter what might be regarded as eccentric spellings of everyday names. We have even been accused of being accentist – a charge we refute with vigour but no conviction. What should be borne in mind is that when we are reliant on the aural word, the only spelling of a name with which we may feel confident is that which would be suggested by the most frequent user of the name. So, for example, the second son of Phil and Jill cannot be called other than Dayveed. Some of these are set out below for the benefit of the obtuse. The other terms with which some people will be unfamiliar are the affectionate names by which Anarchists know one or two of the characters. With a little thought it will be easy to understand the derivation of these, but since we recognize that you may choose to dip into certain entries before others it may be useful to clarify who's who:

Beddy Tugger	Betty Tucker
Boring Christine	Christine Barford
Damien	The dreaded Daniel Hebden
Dayveed	David Archer
Dr Death	Richard Locke
The Dog Woman	Marjorie Antrobus
Fat Clarrie	Clarrie Grundy

Fat Man Forrest	Tom Forrest
Foghorn	Jill Archer
Handbag Hebden	The late unlamented Mark Hebden
Jaaarn	The late lamented John Archer
Jailbird Carter	Susan Carter
Jeck	Jack Woolley
Lancastrian Tommy	Tommy Archer
Mrs High and Mighty	Jennifer Aldridge
The One-eyed Monster	Mike Tucker (or Mike Tugger to you)
Peeep	Pip Archer
Peggoi	Peggy Woolley
Phallustair Blandvoice	Alistair Lloyd
Poll Doll	The late Polly Perks
Roooth	Ruth Archer
That Fisher Woman (TFW)	Janet Fisher
The Village Bicycle	Caroline Pemberton
Wiwyerm	William Grundy

THE ARCHERS ARE REAL – THERE IS NO CAST!

ACCENTS The plethora of accents in Ambridge is a source of considerable mystery to us all. It would appear that the local Borsetshire twang is actually a lot of accents, many of which are more usually found in all four corners of the country. People who have barely set foot outside the village have different accents from their brothers and sisters who have also led totally isolated lives. Consider that ROY, KATE, DEBBIE, DAYVEED, LANCAS-TRIAN TOMMY, EDDIE and WIWYERM were all born in the village and the extent of the problem becomes apparent.

NELSON has a cut-glass accent that belies the criminal son of the village yokel. Note that anyone with a rural accent always calls the Aldridges, PHIL and FOGHORN, JECK WOOLLEY, etc. 'Mr' or 'Mrs' and they, in turn, condescendingly reply to them using their first names.

ADAM TRAVERS-MACY One of the things people have to realize about Ambridge is that it is the closest Britain gets to some South American state, run by a military junta. Pinochet's Chile was a bowl of roses compared with the number of DISAPPEARED in Ambridge. Adam is one such victim. Begat of Jennifer, then not so MRS HIGH AND MIGHTY Archer, and Mr Paddy Redmond, an Irish farm labourer, Adam has had three fathers, been kidnapped and bitten by an adder, and has unaccountably vanished to unknown parts of the globe. It is extremely suspicious that the only references to him are postcards or birthday cards that he may or may not have sent. BRIAN is not someone to throw his money about so how is it that this youth can spend a seemingly endless number of years 'travelling'? It may be that Brian has murdered him and dumped him in a slurry pit due to his failure to adopt his name. Brian and his stepson certainly didn't get on well when Adam was at home.

ALICE ALDRIDGE Of all the pampered brats emanating from Home Farm, Alice must be the most cosseted – even her larynx is protected from the chore of having to aid speech. Something of an afterthought for her parents, Alice cannot in all honesty be said to have made her mark on the village. But of course her behaviour is exemplary. Like all Ambridge children, regardless of which side of the tracks they come from, she is of the 'speak only when you are spoken to' (if then) variety. It is rare indeed for this child ever to tug at its mother's apron strings or butt in to a conversation.

ARCHERS ADDICTS These are the sworn enemies of all decent Anarchists. They describe themselves as the 'official' fan club for *The Archers*, which means they are in the pockets of the establishment. Numbering several thousand conscripts, each wears a worn-out 1970s anorak with a bit of fake rat fur as its collar. Clearly positioned for the proletarian market they run cruises on ocean-going liners at exorbitant rates. What narks us is that they exist to damage the whole creation that is the Home Service's *The Archers* by encouraging people to meet 'the faces behind the voices and by flogging tacky merchandise which misrepresents the pictures we all have of such hallowed institutions as THE BULL, THE CAT, or Brookfield. They even dare to publish something called the *Borchester Echo*. They exist solely as toadies to the BBC establishment and stand for nothing.

BADGER Stripy was the badger lovingly cared for by animal-loving WIWYERM GRUNDY. Unfortunately, with complete disregard for the law, DAYVEED murdered it and then buried it. Badgers are a protected species, and if CLIVE HORROBIN had been indulging in a bit of light badger baiting, the whole village would have gone ape. And was Dayveed completely let off? Is the Pope a Catholic?

BARKING Although most of the population of Ambridge are completely barking, you hear very little dog noise for a rural community. Admittedly, THE DOG WOMAN is generally heralded by a smattering of Afghan baying, but people seem to be able to barge into each other's farms with gay abandon. Anybody who has tried to go within a hundred yards of most farms will know that you have to run the serious risk of being torn limb from limb. Why are dogs so docile in Ambridge?

BEDDY TUGGER This workhorse is in a permanent state of worry and is one of many Ambridge folk who spends her whole life shouting in a rather breathy way. To be fair, life isn't easy for the poor woman. For a start she is married to THE ONE-EYED MONSTER. A few years back it was suggested that Mike might be about to become violent and Beddy fled to THE BULL with the kids. She was on the verge of striking up a non-platonic liaison with SID PERKS, but sadly common sense prevailed.

Beddy was in the village shop on the fateful day that CLIVE HORROBIN and his friend called in to arrange an unsecured loan from the post office. Owing to a totally understandable mix-up, Clive ended up taking the money without asking first. DEBBIE

ALDRIDGE, and KATE were both in the shop at the time, and instead of saying 'Oh it's all a bit of fuss about nothing' they all raised a great hoo-ha about it and poor Clive became the Ambridge One for a while. Beddy was very un-Christian where poor Clive was concerned and was always resentful whenever he came in to the post office for a stamp or a packet of biscuits for his old mum – all this long after he'd done his time.

Money has been in perpetually short supply in the Tugger household since The One-eyed Monster will always blow any available wonga on a hare-brained 'get rich quick' scheme. It is uncertain how they survive. Beddy always does fairly low-paid menial work – although when she was a cleaner at Home Farm it seems highly likely that she was selling sexual favours to the lecherous BRIAN, and of course working in the post office she will be able to avoid paying for many stamps.

BEETLE BANKS Some dozy idea of DEBBIE ALDRIDGE's which has never been explained. Is it a service for the benefit of beetles wishing to cash cheques without being trodden on or is it an alternative form of currency for us all to use as we eagerly await the Euro?

Bert Fry The most recent in a long and distinguished line of village idiots. Bert is the kind of person who simply doesn't exist, and therefore poses a great challenge to the Anarchist motto. Were a cast to exist, Bert would most certainly be part of it. Bert is essentially the type of person for whom adult literacy classes were intended – which makes it all the more daft that he writes poetry and had the gumption to become a pub quiz cheat. Where we can sympathize with him is in the misery he must endure having to work under DAYVEED and ROOOTH. He must have suffered great humiliation when the cell count was deemed to have fallen because he shouted at the cows. It doesn't really matter if and when Bert dies because he, like the other TOKEN OLD FARMING RETAINERS, will automatically be replaced by someone with an identical voice and character.

BISHOP CYRIL The Bishop of Felpersham has been known to speak in the past. He is only occasionally referred to although he is a mucker of JECK WOOLLEY's. For some reason he seemed to stick his crook into the business of ROBIN STOKES and THE VILLAGE BICYCLE when they were considering tying the knot. Being a wise and intuitive old geezer he presumably realized that it was hardly going to be a match made in heaven to splice together a holy joe with a prospective professional murderess (and an atheist to wit). Anarchist respect for Cyril went into sharp decline when he permitted the installation of the obvious fraudster THAT FISHER WOMAN as the vicarette at St Stephen's. He obviously allowed himself to have the mitre pulled well and truly over his eyes and should have listened to PEGGOI who did her best to prevent the whole business.

BORCHESTER FEED MILLS They must have a strange commission system since they were prepared to employ complete divots such as NEIL CARTER who has about as much sales acumen as a bag of pig nuts. On the other hand they also employed a silent bloke called Derek whose legendary sales abilities were forever being rammed down poor Neil's throat at one time. Neil was right to quit, because when a mute is beating you at sales you really have to accept you may not have found your true vocation.

BORING CHRISTINE Although part of our anarchic creed is to gainsay the existence of actors, we have to make an honourable exception in the case of Christine. Her whole being revolves around reading lines in such a manner as to sound as if

she is permanently on stage in one of the loathed VILLAGE PRO-
DUCTIONS. Whatever she says is uniformly without conviction.
Aged in her late 60s she has a deceptively young voice and has a
couple of fine hours of note in her history. In the mid-1950s her
horse was kindly contributing to a barbecue, presumably for
some French people, when busybody GRACE ARCHER offered
to take its place. Then in summer1997 she was at the centre of
the great vomit in the duckpond party at the village hall, throwing her weight around left, right and centre and carefully picking
up bits of broken glass and diced carrot.

Newer listeners should bear in mind that she drove her first
husband, businessman Paul Johnson, to a nervous breakdown. So
tortured was he by the pressure exerted on him by the Archer
mafia that he crashed his car on the German autobahn. Mystery
surrounds the fate of their adopted son Peter. He is barely mentioned by Christine, never apparently visits, and no one ever asks
her about him. Clearly another of THE DISAPPEARED.

Christine is only really interested in horses, which is just as
well as horses are the only creatures likely to be interested in
her. Her reaction when GEORGE was allegedly attacked last year
was, by any standard, bizarre. She exclaimed, 'Oh why did it have
to happen on a Tuesday?' We all accept that Tuesday is a damned
inconvenient time to have your husband beaten up, but surely it
wouldn't be at the forefront of the mind of a truly loving wife.
When Christine was a Johnson they lived at Wynfords Farm
which had to be sold to pay off debts. Who on earth bought it,
because it's never been mentioned since? Perhaps the Americans
bought it to put next to London Bridge in the Arizona Desert.
The awful SHULA still persists in calling her 'Auntie Chris' which
is quite grotesque at their ages.

BRENDA TUGGER Brenda has done little in what has been
a more or less silent existence. She spoke briefly when she was

involved with a bunch of village hooligans terrorizing Ambridge under the careful stewardship of KATE but has subsequently taken the normal vows. She is the sort of girl for whom a permanent voice could do wonders.

BRIAN ALDRIDGE The village owes Brian a huge debt of gratitude as he is the only serious, job-creating entrepreneur in Ambridge. He has been plagued with problems over the years – being married to MRS HIGH AND MIGHTY, being seduced by THE VILLAGE BICYCLE, having the drippy, directionless DEBBIE perpetually moaning on about not being kept informed.

Brian has stoically fought his epilepsy and runs a thoroughly successful series of farming enterprises. He is forever having to fend off woolly environmentalists and do-gooders but he persists with the right attitudes. Brian knows that the best thing to do with a public footpath is plough over it and hope everyone forgets it was there. Hedgerows are for wooftahs and pesticides get rid of pests – although sadly not all of them.

Sad as we were when HARDWORKING SIMON left us, we were delighted when Brian formed a consortium with Borchester Land and the excellent MATT CRAWFORD to buy the Estate. With a bit of luck he'll whack up the rents on the tenanted farms and perhaps we can at last have a decent supermarket in the village.

Brian is all man and likes a bit of female variety in his life. He enjoyed his fling with The Village Bicycle and also took a great interest in the Pony Club, where he had another fling with one Mandy Beesborough. The best thing about Brian is that he has a first-class sarcastic sense of humour, a quality to be treasured in a dour village like Ambridge.

BSE ANDY An old college friend of ROOOTH'S for whom she clearly carried not only a torch but also a child. Andy's farming specialities were very much in the area of tallow, bulls' semen and other derivatives and he was therefore hit rather hard by the BSE fiasco. If he'd gone in for FLAX this would never have been a problem. Roooth and Andy met again at a reunion – not attended by DAYVEED – shortly after which she announced her pregnancy. Dayveed appears not to have noticed the coincidence of the dates, but when Josh suddenly metamorphoses into a hamburger the dreadful secret will out.

BULL, THE At the heart of any English village is its local pub. SID PERKS has run The Bull for over 25 years, although strangely no one (himself included) seemed to notice that 1997 was his silver jubilee there.

The great mystery is that its fortunes have gone downhill as villagers seem to have deserted it in favour of THE CAT. As far as we can tell, Sid has basically maintained the friendly rural character of the pub and although some of the restaurant ventures seem to have bombed out it seems quite ludicrous that so many people prefer the camp cuisine of SEAN MYERSON. Even more out of character is that the only time any decent quantity of people shows up is for the boules nights, another manifestation of DIWALI-itis.

It should be noted that ownership of The Bull now resides jointly between THE VILLAGE BICYCLE and the Perkses. The Village Bicycle, who used to work there, occasionally makes suggestions as to how to improve business. but generally doesn't seem to give a toss. She seems to prefer to compete against her own enterprise by working at GREY GABLES.

The main problem with The Bull is that KATHY PERKS has a pathological hatred of customers, pubs and cooking. When a landlady of a pub utters the immortal words 'I try and go in the bar as little as possible' you know there is a problem. In contrast the desperate Sid clings to the old-fashioned notion of giving good service, which is why he irritatingly says things like 'all part of the service' when someone just so much as thanks him for their change. Sid went into apoplexy when Sean tentatively sounded Caroline out with the possibility of turning The Bull pink, though even she was having none of that. But unless Sid can enter into a proper working partnership with someone who actually wants to make a go of the place things don't look too good for the future of The Bull.

C

CAMERON FRASER A Scottish person who owned the estate before HARDWORKING SIMON, he was a good warm-up act for Simon because he too was one of those people who actually wanted to run the whole thing like a business. Indeed he was so keen on business that he acquired various amounts of investment from the more gullible members of the village including THE VILLAGE BICYCLE (amusingly) and THE DOG WOMAN (sadly). The Village Bicycle was only too keen to justify her epithet with Mr Fraser until he became more interested in ELIZABETH. Cameron led daft Lizzie a merry dance, finally inflicting the cruelest punishment that anyone could imagine – leaving her at a motorway service station. It was no thanks to him that she was eventually rescued from a potential life sentence of over-priced, over-cooked food, and people with tattoos playing space invaders. People always tend to speak ill of entrepreneurs after they've gone, (just look at the things they say about that nice Mr Maxwell) so you can take with a pinch of salt those who say Cameron Fraser was a crook. Given the lawless nature of Ambridge folk, it is very much a case of pots and kettles. We can only hope that one day he will return to clear his tarnished name.

CAPTAIN The late beloved dog of JECK WOOLLEY was found dead by GEORGE (ALCOPOP) BARFORD – by no means the first time the words 'dog' and 'dead' have followed in close proximity when George is around. No one seems to have tumbled to the coincidence.

CASTISM The most mortal sin known to man. Physical manifestations include bottles of SHIRES beer, MARTHA

WOODFORD's cookbooks and people claiming to be characters from *The Archers*. Metaphysical manifestations include comments such as 'What are they going to do now the actor who plays NELSON's died?' or 'Did you know that HAYLEY is the daughter of Jasper Carrot?' The main perpetrators of this heinous crime are insensitive people at Pebble Mill, certain misguided newspaper journalists (particularly in the *Radio Times*) and of course the dreaded Archers Addicts. In the unlikely event that anyone should challenge our motto 'The Archers are real – there is no cast!' we have only to point out to them the appearances over the years from the likes of showjumper Anne Moore, Princess Margaret, Lord Lichfield and Britt Eckland. Come on Anoraks – who 'plays' them?

CAT AND FIDDLE, THE Before the teenage brat pack got hold of it, The Cat and Fiddle was the noble watering hole of such distinguished luminaries as Baggy and Snatch Foster. It was also the place where the layabout Grundys always seemed happiest in the days before they joined the establishment. Predominantly patronized by lager drinkers, The Cat was a haven where characters could escape from the establishment figures who were perpetual bar flies at THE BULL. It was run by a succession of n'ere-do-wells until the day that SEAN MYERSON and his partner Peter took it over and turned it into an incongruously trendy place. On a bad night you can almost hear the silly piece of lime sticking out of a bottle of San Miguel and going up some spotty teenager's nose.

At times we have wondered whether or not The Cat is actually a caravan since it seems to move around considerably. Sometimes it is within earshot of SID's homophobic remarks, whilst other days it can be well on the way to Felpersham. The introduction of wide-screen television just about encapsulates the utter vulgarity of the place.

CELL COUNT This is a subject that has come up a few times in recent years, especially when ROOOTH said that the cell count in Brookfield's milk was falling because BERT kept shouting at the cows. Apparently you get the best milk by moaning quietly but interminably in a strong Geordie accent.

CLIFF-HANGER Not a character but a much lamented institution that Anarchists would like to see revived. More long-in-the-tooth listeners will remember that in the good old days each nightly episode would end with a little cliff-hanger. It would be something of the ilk of WALTER GABRIEL calling out 'NELSON, Nelson', there being no reply, Walter exclaiming 'Oh no', and the signature tune cutting in. In those days we didn't have car radios so the next day we'd be double de-clutching like there was no tomorrow to get home on time to hear the outcome. In the event the 'Oh no' would have been because one of Walter's marrows had exploded, but it had us on tenterhooks overnight.

On a Friday, it was the real business with a mega cliff-hanger to stop us ditching the Home Service over the weekend and deserting to The Light Programme. This would be the great Ambridge mail van robbery or something with a bit of meat in it. Nowadays there is no proper structure. Cataclysmic announcements are as likely to come in the middle of the programme on a Monday as at any other time. JAAARN's death, which must rank as one of the most harrowing events in the history of *The Archers*, happened on a Wednesday. We are forever treated to soppy endings like THAT FISHER WOMAN saying, 'Happy Easter to you all.' Where is the oomph?

CLIVE HORROBIN Clive has been dealt a real bum rap in many respects. First, he was unlucky in love. Despite his best efforts he has been unable to keep his relationship with SHARON together. He desperately misses his daughter KYLIE and should be given proper access to her. He was then unfortunately mixed up in an overblown incident in the village shop which was all a big fuss about nothing. He simply took some money without asking first, and waved a gun at BEDDY TUGGER in an amusing and playful little gesture. Normal people would have laughed it off but of course Beddy had to go and involve the police, as if they didn't have better things to do.

Clive had the good sense to keep away while he was on remand, and he was simply doing this because he realized how much taxpayers' money it costs to keep people in prison, so thought he would do everyone a favour by fending for himself. JAILBIRD was most ungracious when it came to giving her brother a helping hand, and he ended up back inside. Anarchists were delighted when in summer 1997, Clive returned to Ambridge having done his time and more than paying his debt to society. One or two people, notably THE ONE-EYED MONSTER made various threats against him, but LYNDA SNELL who recognizes that the establishment tend to have a downer on people for no good reason was very helpful in rehabilitating him.

Poor Clive was of course immediately under suspicion whenever some dozy cow mislaid their purse, but being the good-natured chap that he is, he always took it on the chin. It would have been a heartless cur indeed who did not feel sympathy for Clive when he was fitted up for a minor assault on GEORGE (ALCOPOP) BARFORD – as if Clive would be interested in dead deer. Talk about circumstantial evidence, the establishment were desperate to pin this one on him and were relying on abstruse points of nonsense such as George's watch turning up on Sharon's wrist. The treatment and lack of regard for Clive sits in sharp contrast with the acceptance of former armed robber NELSON GABRIEL or the adulation constantly heaped upon murderer FAT MAN FORREST over the years. Clive's day will come. We must have patience.

COUNCIL HOUSES We don't know how many people live in the council houses nor even how many houses there are. We know SHARON and KYLIE lived in one. When they left it was then occupied by some people about whom we know only one thing: that they were annoyed when JAAARN went round to see if the errant SINGLE WICKET TROPHY was still lurking from the days when he used to live there. We can safely assume that the Horrobins live in one, but as far as we know the only other people who live in municipal housing are the elderly folk who live in MANORFIELD CLOSE.

CRAVEN There is nothing we can say of Craven to distinguish him from SPANNER. He seemed to have exactly the same attributes and shortcomings. Indeed they were probably Siamese twins.

CRICKET The village cricket team is a constant source of acrimony and the nearest we ever get to team spirit is a pink gin at THE CAT after a match. Rather like VILLAGE PRODUCTIONS, the desire of anyone to participate in the team always works in direct inverse to their ability. Thus duffers like Eddie are always trying to get in the team, and the better players always fail to turn up to 'nets'. Under the captaincy of Saint SEAN MYERSON, team selection seems to have become an even more bitter affair. Yet it is quite remarkable that despite Sean's ultra serious approach he is prepared to tolerate Bert Fry as an umpire, complete with his pre-senile dementia. There is a strange lack of interest in national cricket. We never hear any discussion of test or even county matches and no one goes to watch their local side.

CUCKOO A cuckoo used to arrive in Ambridge around April and be heard in every outdoor scene until July. In 1997 and 1998 it was not heard at all. This was doubtless due to excessive cropspraying by non-organic farmers.

D

DAMIEN Anyone who is familiar with the film *Omen* will realize that the child-creature begat of SHULA and a test tube is a child of the Devil. The sight of her, PHALLUSTAIR, DR DEATH, *et al.* desperately wondering what was wrong with him was pitiful indeed, yet we knew that the only real solution lay in a metal stake, a cross and a good supply of organic garlic from the farm shop. There have been so many signs that he is not of this earth that it is just amazing no one else has noticed. One minute he speaks in clipped Oxford tones, the next he reverts to demonic gurgling. He has demonstrated the attitude of a spoilt brat, but any old fool can see that he has something of the night about him. He has developed an unnatural habit of answering all questions using full sentences. When his fangs are fully grown no one in the village will be safe.

DAN ARCHER During his long life, Dan was the proud owner of no less than four radically different voices. He was a pioneer of Archer cosiness and he and his old bat of a wife DORIS spent their latter days clucking away in just the same self-congratulatory manner as FOGHORN and PHIL do today. Since the most unpleasant criminals are often the people you least expect, it must be odds on that Dan cunningly hid a very dubious side to his nature. It would not do to delve too deeply into the activities he got up to with Blossom and Boxer, nor should we ask too many questions about their demise. Dan had a vicious side to him – he was very unforgiving toward his younger brother Ben who had attempted to go the distance with young Doris and the poor bloke was banished to one of the colonies. Like many people in Ambridge, Dan was more or less murdered. ELIZABETH was driving him when they spotted a sheep that needed a helping hand, as sheep so often do. Given a choice between the young healthy Elizabeth or frail 90-year-old Dan, there was no contest as to who should go to the rescue. So good old Lizzie sat in the car while Dan went twelve rounds with the sheep. Needless to say, the sheep won, and Elizabeth picked up a few quid in the will.

DAN ARCHER NUCLEAR TESTING SITE Known to the cosies as The DAN ARCHER Memorial Playground, this was another 'pass the sick bucket' establishment idea in which a sub-committee set up an unnecessary facility for a village in which there are hardly any children. Prominent members of the Committee included: BORING CHRISTINE (well past child-bearing age and wasn't able to have children anyway when she was young – she has also lost her adopted son which is rather careless); SHULA (always dumped DAMIEN on her mother anyway, until he became possessed in spring 1998), and USHA GUPTA (certainly can't begin to think about children until Auntie Satia and brother SHIFFON have arranged a nice marriage for her). We were right behind JOE when he objected to the name for the playground. His own dear wife Susan was just as worthy of a memorial, and we felt it would have been rather more appropriate to have named it after Bob Larkin, the poor soul murdered by FAT MAN FORREST. The white elephant was duly built and is now never mentioned.

DAVE BARRY A policeman and an all-round good bloke. The problem is that everyone in Ambridge is suspicious of policemen, so Dave was only ever really liked by KATHY, who was particularly partial to his truncheon. Like JIM COVERDALE and various passing policemen since, Dave's crime was to try to turn in criminals, in his case NELSON and, as usual, EDDIE. Ambridge is a bit like the Maze Prison as far as law and order is concerned. Police are only allowed into the village when invited, and strictly on the condition that they turn a blind eye to any crime.

DAYVEED ARCHER (MURDERER) Listeners will all know that DAYVEED has a bit of a temper on him – and who wouldn't have, being married to the Geordie gorgon, ROOOTH. But newer listeners and those with defective memories may not realize that Dayveed should be locked up and the key thrown away. Back in the mid 1980s he was cutting down a TREE BRANCH with faithful retainer Jethro Larkin (a man who had never harmed anyone) when he allowed the branch to fall 'accidentally' on his head and kill him. Poor Jethro was a goner and this can only have been good news for Dayveed who often complained at the poor man for being a bit slow in his old age. Dayveed got off scot-free and of course there were no witnesses apart from a few million listeners. If there were any justice in the world, Dayveed would have been successfully prosecuted on a manslaughter charge. An effective establishment cover-up yet again, just like the BADGER. More recently Dayveed led a bloodthirsty spade attack on a family of innocent rats, commenting, 'It's years since I had a good rat hunt.' His blood lust is palpable.

Dayveed has no sense of humour. He never relaxes and is one of those people who makes you feel guilty about enjoying yourself. He is always too busy to do anything except farming, and yet during the glorious Pemberton era he took on a whole chunk of Estate land without apparently increasing staff. He has a good shout on him and we all enjoy it when he blows his top.

DEBBIE ALDRIDGE She has the distinction of being the only person in the village to have had three surnames (Travers-Macy, Macy, Aldridge) without being married. In fact, probably the only person in the world.

Debbie finds it impossible to strike up normal relationships with men and shows all the signs of having had a very disturbed childhood. She is a real drifter, the kind of person who if she was not bank-rolled by her parents would probably be sitting in a council house watching television game shows all day.

She went to Exeter University but blew that because of a relationship with some bloke. She got involved with antiques for a while in a very dodgy partnership with crook NELSON and since then has flitted around the farm working for Daddy. Debbie is constantly moaning about not being consulted on decision making, but then a hard-nosed businessman like BRIAN is hardly going to confide in some know-nothing who will start blabbing around if she doesn't agree with him. Brian realizes that the way to deal with his stepdaughter is to say 'of course I'll consult you' every now and then, but then just go off and do his own thing. She even went as far as claiming to have been offered some job in advertising in London. This was obviously a phantom offer because when Brian trotted out his usual line Debbie decided to stay at home.

Debbie had a fling with DR DEATH at one stage but seems to have developed a liking for the Lady Chatterley role. She appeared to go the distance with Steve Oakley, a farm hand who later gave her the old heave-ho. Her liaison with HARDWORKING SIMON gave her father some hope that he may at last get her off his hands. Sadly she got all upset about Simon's plan to introduce a bit of FLAX at Grange Farm and cut off sexual relations on the strength of it. This culminated in the unfortunate RIDING ACCIDENT. What's the betting she'll go for the real Mellors, the affable GREG TURNER? On the other hand you can get decent odds on a short-lived link-up with PHALLUSTAIR.

DEMON DRINK Ambridge has had more than its fair share of inebriates over the years, which is a realistic characteristic much enjoyed by Anarchists. Grade-one boozers would have to include Jack Archer who died of it and GEORGE (ALCOPOP) BARFORD and his former live-in lover Nora Macauley who were both forced to sign the pledge. JOAN PARGETTER could put it away until she went on the wagon with unlikely ease. Another is LILLIAN, although we have not heard from her for ages and don't know how she's getting on with the sherbets at the moment. Serious drinkers who don't mess around include the Grundys, TONY ARCHER and LANCASTRIAN TOMMY.

DISAPPEARED, THE There are essentially two categories of disappeared – those who are mentioned but never appear and those whose names never pass anyone's lips. Most of the second classification are barely mentioned in this book which just shows that the establishment has even succeeded in brainwashing *us!* THE TREGORRANS seem to have left behind no friends in Ambridge and the same can be said of Hugo Barnaby and many others. We never hear of Harry and Marilyn Booker. They allegedly live in Penny Hassett yet no one ever bumps into them in Borchester. PAT never mentions, or visits, her Uncle Haydn in Wales although he lived in the village long before she turned up and would presumably like to come and see old friends. Most children of Ambridge residents never come to visit their parents, nor do their parents visit them. Another sinister aspect to the whole business is that newcomers to the village generally have no past, and no relations. We can only conclude that they are someone else's disappeared. The key question is whether Ambridge's disappeared ever left the village. The answer is almost certainly that they didn't – there has to be some explanation for TONY and Pat's rich organic soil.

DIWALI This is an ancient Borsetshire festival, revived by SHIFFON GUPTA, which cheered up the whole village – even DR DEATH – in a way that boring old Guy Fawkes night could never do. A few glasses of carrot juice and a vegetable samosa and everyone was well away.

DR DEATH (MURDERER) There are relatively few intruders from the outside world, and when they enter Ambridge it is as if they are joining a closed order. Dr Death appears to have no relations. Indeed he may not even be a real doctor. When he arrived he was known for being a Sealed Knot anorak, yet this is rarely referred to nowadays. He has presumably fallen victim to a strange affliction in Ambridge which is the sudden abandonment of a hobby which had apparently dominated one's whole existence (PHIL's cooking is a similar example). Dr Death is without question a murderer. He clearly gave old MRS BARRACLOUGH a little helping hand, and few of us were surprised to learn that she had 'remembered' him in her will. Locke has been pretty quiet about just how much he was left or what he has done with it, but he was certainly given a fright when MR BARRACLOUGH rightly got the GMC on the case. It transpired that the 'Dr' had failed to keep proper notes. Given the way he slobs around in the cottage he shares with USHA, it is likely that he maintains a poor standard of cleanliness where his implements are concerned.

Before Usha, Locke first set his stethoscope at DEBBIE. Presumably he thought that she might be a good financial bet, this being before he discovered Mrs B. The problem with Debbie is that she is so screwed up where men are concerned that although she led him on, she wasn't prepared to go for gold. And it was typical of her that she was miffed when he set up shop with Usha. The coupling of Dr Death and Usha is odd indeed and they are surely cruisin' for a bruisin'. Doctors tend not to stay too long in Ambridge, and it's time he went, and a real, qualified doctor took his place.

Dr Death is always happy to chat about his cases to any old Tom, Dick or Harry and regards the Hypocratic Oath as a darned

THE ARCHERS ARE REAL – THERE IS NO CAST!

nuisance. It is noted that he makes a huge number of house calls, almost always to women. He does this with an enthusiasm quite unparalleled in his profession who usually feel that the only reasonable grounds on which they should be expected to visit a patient's house is to issue a death certificate. More recently Dr Death has rogered the dreaded SHULA. His unhealthy interest in her while DAMIEN was waiting for his exorcism had led rapidly to an uncontrolled snog. SHULA, with her unsavoury record of blackmail, will be able to hold the threat of the GMC over him for years to come. In due course the serial seductress will demand prescriptions at will as DAMIEN becomes ever more crazed.

DOG WOMAN, THE We like Marjorie Antrobus because she has the ability to be free of malice yet not be sanctimonious. She is a lonely lady who has done a lot for the village – not least in offering 'no strings attached' cooking and accommodation to some of the dullest menfolk in Borsetshire. If she didn't surround herself with smelly Afghans, she would be a true saint.

Marjorie brings the spirit of the Raj to our multicultural village. You can almost hear the sound of her late husband Teddy's rifle as another tiger bites the dust. She is a true toff and yet she does not despise the riffraff. During her years in the village, The Dog Woman has had a number of platonic relationships with gentlemen of the old school – Colonel Freddie Danby and Rev. Gerry Buckle come to mind. She's always quite keen on vicars and if we have one quarrel with her, it is for tolerating THAT FISHER WOMAN. One of her particularly endearing qualities is the rather peculiar inflexion she uses when someone offends her. Look out for it.

DOORS CLOSING All doors in Ambridge sound exactly the same (even the FOGHORN's Aga ones) when they close. Now how could that be?

DORIS ARCHER We know what you're thinking – 'Doris Archer was a goddess, Ambridge's Queen Mum. No one, but no one can have a word to say against her, surely?' We're almost scared to comment in case some of the sadder listeners send us poison-pen letters or set fire to our HQ. The truth is that Doris was as boring as hell. She was all jam and cooking and recipes and giving milk to obstinate little lambs that couldn't be bothered to find their mums, and dishing out pseudo 'wise' words. Why is it that when people become old they are described as 'wise'? What generally happens is that we go gaga, and Doris was just the same. By far the worst thing she did was to bequeath her home, Glebe Cottage, to SHULA of all people. Just how divisive can you get? She had seven grandchildren plus BORING CHRISTINE's Peter but she still left her house to the dreaded Shula. And we'll give you one guess as to who 'found' her dead in an armchair – yep, you've got it, Shula.

DUCKS Once in a while it is remembered that Ambridge has a VILLAGE POND, and therefore ducks. Small children allegedly feed them – ALICE, the dreaded DAMIEN, PEEEP, etc. And of course LANCASTRIAN TOMMY thoughtfully fed them in 1997. But otherwise they go months, sometimes years without a mention. Now that the village is so cosmopolitan, it's only a matter of time before a Chinese family moves in, and then it will be curtains for the ducks.

E

EDDIE GRUNDY Some years ago there was a fine and worthy organization called 'The Eddie Grundy Fan Club'. It owed its success to the fact that the Grundys in general and Eddie in particular were reviled by the cosy establishment figures, notably the Archer clan.

There are two clear explanations for the demise of that august body. First, it was an overtly CASTIST organization and used to delight in parading absurd people who claimed to be characters from *The Archers* at its 'Eddie ups'. Second, Eddie has gradually become an accepted bastion of the slightly-disestablished establishment. If an equivalent organization were to be formed today it would have to centre on CLIVE HORROBIN or someone of that ilk.

Anarchists have long since ceased regarding Eddie as the rebel we would like him to be. Gone are the days when he sought to improve the tone of the piano in THE BULL with the injection of a large quantity of diced carrot. It's not entirely his fault, but he has been all too ready to fawn at the feet of the ghastly SHULA – for example, when he wanted help over his threatened eviction from Grange Farm. Eddie has even passed up the opportunity to play away with THE LILY OF LAYTON CROSS.

There is a great mystery surrounding the running of Grange Farm. Though it is clearly no gold mine, it does seem to be a working farm with crops and animals, specializing of course in turkeys. They employ no staff, and JOE appears to do virtually no work, which is nowadays forgivable since he is in his late 70s. FAT CLARRIE toils at Bridge Farm making PC yogurt, and serves in The Bull at night, so she is not doing any work at Grange Farm. This leaves Eddie to run the place single-handed. Yet he is endlessly pestering neighbouring farmers for work. How does he do it? He is either a workaholic or an excellent time manager.

EDWARD GRUNDY One of the serried ranks of THE DISAPPEARED, Edward's name is always prefaced by the word 'and' as in 'WIWYERM and Edward'. He did sing 'Once in Royal David's City' at the Ambridge carol service in 1995 with a voice that made King's College choristers sound decidedly second rate. Whether he still lives is a moot point. Unlike his brother, it is hard to say that he has ever really done anything. The one thing we have heard about him is the odd intimation that he felt a bit miffed at THE VILLAGE BICYCLE lavishing bikes and cows on his brother all the time. It is quite possible that since EDDIE, Wiwyerm and JOE all have an eye for a few quid on a shady deal, Edward has been sold to slavery. Certainly FAT CLARRIE is so gullible and bonkers that it would be easy enough to spin her some yarn to explain his prolonged absence, whilst at the same time getting over a politically correct point: 'He's gone into Borchester love, and you know how bad the rural bus services are nowadays.'

ELIZABETH PARGETTER One of the Archer brats, now in her 30s. If you want to know what she used to be like you need look no further than KATE. She too was all veggie and Lefty in her youth. She failed any significant educational challenges that came her way and took up a career of picking up SHULA's discarded boyfriends, sandwiched between a whole series of unsuitable blokes on the way. On a slight deviation from this path, she took one of THE VILLAGE BICYCLE's boyfriends, CAMERON FRASER, and he managed to get her up the duff before abandoning her at a motorway service station and doing a runner off the face of the earth. Unlike Kate, Elizabeth decided she did not want to bring up a sprog, and ended the pregnancy. This, of course, went down like a pork pie at a bar mitzvah with Shula who is absolutely nuts about children and seemed to think that her sister should have gone into the surrogacy business for her.

When Elizabeth decided to marry, she chose another of Shula's discards, the loopy ex-ice-cream and swimming-pool salesman NIGEL PARGETTER. Nigel has only ever really fancied Shula and still does, but he has obviously regarded Elizabeth as the nearest he is going to get, whilst still keeping a foot in the door. Elizabeth has never really been head over heels for Nigel but saw an opportunity to get some unearned wonga by grasping hold of LOWER LOXLEY, Nigel's ancestral home.

Elizabeth's treatment of her mother-in-law has been nothing short of scandalous. From the day she married Nigel she has sought to edge poor JOAN ever further into oblivion. During Christmas 1997 she went to the most amazing lengths to ensure that Joan would not spend the festive period at Lower Loxley (by taking over the complete management of NELSON's wine bar to enable him to keep her away). She seems to have forgotten that Lower Loxley is actually Joan's home.

One of the mysteries for a while was how Elizabeth was apparently earning large fees for lecturing in courses on public relations. As far as we could see, her only experience in this field was management of a struggling third-rate conference centre, where all the work was done by Nigel anyway. We soon realized that she was actually earning fees as a high-class hooker to satisfy the near insatiable appetite of HORNY HUGH. Of course she denied it, but you would wouldn't you? There are disturbing signs that she might now be thinking of getting herself in the family way – a ghastly notion that will herald the arrival of more gooey-cooey grandmotherly nonsense from the FOGHORN.

ELLIE MAY Thankfully we hear far fewer lovey dovey scenes between Elizabeth and Nigel than we used to, but the most vomit-provoking moments always surrounded the fuss they made over their pet cow. It is of course quite absurd that a farmer's grown-up non-farming daughter would be given a cow as a wedding present. Anarchists were furious that she was spared when the BSE issue was at its height. We have always yearned to hear of Ellieburgers and there was a wonderful moment when she seemed set for an early trip to the butcher. Unfortunately she was reprieved and even used for breeding.

EMMA CARTER We know very little about her except that she used to wet the bed when she was worried about having a JAILBIRD for a mother. She also began taking things from the village shop without asking first, specializing in sanitary towels. And why shouldn't she? It was only something she picked up from her uncle. The good thing about Emma is that she introduced the name 'DR DEATH' for our loathsome doctor. She'd heard it mentioned in the playground at the time of the scandal of MRS BARRACLOUGH's death.

A couple of years back Emma was being bullied at school by Karen. Typically of the PC *Archers*, instead of expelling Karen or giving her six of the best, they had a policy of being nice to her and before we knew it Emma was a guest at Karen's house being plied with hot doughnuts. Perhaps we should have tried this tack with Adolf Hitler – we might have averted a world war.

ERIC The pig that HAYLEY and LANCASTRIAN TOMMY purchased on the rebound from JAAARN's death has caused a number of highly distasteful scenes which we hardly wish to discuss in a family book. Hayley seems obsessed with talking about Eric's sexual habits and when we were told that his wedding tackle had been damaged through putting it where it 'oughtn't to be' – well, really. The final straw was when NEIL said they were going to have to help him put it in the 'right' place.

ℱ

FAT CLARRIE In the good old days before political correctness took its stranglehold, there used to be readings on *Listen with Mother* about 'Big Fat Rosie'. The voice used to portray the character was exactly the same as that of Clarrie. She has to wander around Ambridge sounding like some halfwit. It is quite obvious that she is a lump of lard, and why EDDIE settled for her when he could have had THE LILY OF LAYTON CROSS is baffling. But we like Clarrie. She is entirely without malice, whilst at the same time she is a beast of great burden. She is, of course, completely gullible which is why she is always prepared to think the best of her family of wasters. It was typical that when JOE and Eddie were trying to flog the boys' World Cup tickets, Clarrie was the only person in the village who didn't know about it. She is infinitely nicer than JAILBIRD because she has accepted her rightful place at the bottom of the pile.

FAT MAN FORREST (MURDERER) The thing that many people forget about dear old Uncle Tom is that he is a murderer. Some years ago he shot and killed Bob Larkin who was allegedly poaching. More to the point, and for some unaccountable reason, Bob had his eye on PRU (this was before Tom and Pru were married), and it was highly coincidental that Tom should 'accidentally' kill him. Unsurprisingly the village establishment closed ranks and backed Tom. He was acquitted in a court case redolent of the justice system of some banana republic.

In 1996, evidence came to light to suggest he may be a war criminal. A German bomber was dug up in the village with the pilot still in it. Tom seemed to know about the crash so why didn't he rescue the poor hun?

Fat Man Forrest has often been one of the stomach-churningly cosy characters, always poking his nose into other people's business, always ready with a disapproving view on things, and boring beyond measure. His tendency to sing *The Village Pump* is to be deplored, and happily seems to have subsided, though he did muster some tuneless old folk song at Christmas 1997. He is now 88, and at times has been quite gaga. But in Ambridge, all gaga people suffer from 'Saundersism' – a rare condition that renders the sufferer completely incapable one minute, and like a contestant on *Round Britain Quiz* just a few moments later.

Like his wife, Tom now resides in THE LAURELS, but still emerges to hold thoroughly lucid conversations, with barely a discernible 'um' or 'er'. He almost sounds like an actor. Fat Man Forrest has the distinction of being one of those few characters who has moved from being detested by Anarchists to being quietly respected by us. This is mainly due to the fact that he has gone from being nauseatingly cosy to being a cantankerous old bar steward. He is crotchety, unreasonable and negative about everything. He winds up the likes of FOGHORN, MRS HIGH AND MIGHTY, BORING CHRISTINE and SHULA. For all this he has our admiration. But at the end of the day he is a murderer and should be treated as such, the right place for Tom is not The Laurels but Winson Green.

FEATHERS, THE A posh place out of the village where some of the nobs go when they want to get their ends away. Whilst the place gets no mention for years on end, if a character ever does go there, they inevitably meet someone else from Ambridge who they are wanting to avoid.

FERGIE, THE Considering it was only a tractor, The Fergie really did play a starring role over a period of time. It was falsely accused of murdering poor JAAARN, yet we all know that it was not really to blame. Earlier it had been accused of nearly causing TONY to get involved in a little extracurricular activity with a weird girl called Sandy who had a particularly unhealthy interest in old tractors. After JAAARN's death, Tony exiled it to some Fergie museum which we can assume is the tractorial equivalent of THE LAURELS. It is ironic that the dreaded Archers Anoraks calendar showed Tony lovingly tending his Fergie in June 1998, some months after he had disposed of it.

15 MINUTES This is the standard answer to the question 'How long is a daily episode of *The Archers*?' It is also completely untrue. It has to share the space with the news, adverts for other radio (and even television) programmes and blatant commercials for the dreaded Archers Addicts. Sadly, the programme is now some meaningless and variable length.

FLAX Had HARDWORKING SIMON had his way, Grange Farm would now boast a fine crop of flax. Sadly, the cosy establishment weighed in and prevented him from kicking out the Grundys. So if it's flax you want you'll have to go elsewhere.

FLOWER AND PRODUCE SHOW, THE This is a good event that always manages to create genuine acrimony and adds nicely to the sum of human misery. There is generally some rivalry over the quality of jam on show or the size of marrows. Unfortunately some of the great protagonists are now themselves part of the fertilizer – WALTER, FAT MAN FORREST (virtually), PRU (virtually), BERT FRY (voice now too silly).

A village has to have a super-cook, someone who enters every class at the show and expects to win as if it is their birthright. Nowadays this is the silent FREDA FRY. Having a husband with such an absurd voice is obviously something of a deterrent to having a voice herself so she throws her weight into produce manufacturing. The judges used to be people of stature, but now it's as likely as not to be TFW. How times have changed.

FOGHORN Where would we be without Jill? A darn site happier. Not to put too fine a point on it – she sucks. She is the epitome of cosiness. Jill is to the fore in those dreadful episodes where the 12 minutes have elapsed but nothing has happened. It's been 12 minutes of Jill saying, 'Aren't we lucky Phil?' and 'If only your mother could have seen little Daniel,' and 'I'm worried about SHULA, she didn't have a third cup of tea this morning when she called round,' and 'Do you know it's our 300th wedding anniversary and it only seems like yesterday. Come over here and give me a kiss,' and 'I've made plenty of supper if another six million people would like to come round into our warm cosy ...' Urgh, urgh, urgh. Please pass the sick bucket.

FOGHORN ... AGAIN We had to break off the last entry to get a pint of milk of magnesia but there is more to be said about Jill. Early in 1998 she suddenly 'came out' as a business expert. After years of saying 'yes sir, no sir, three bags full sir' to her dreary beloved husband, she temporarily took on a mind of her own and supported DAYVEED and ROOOTH in their plans to expand the cow herd. PHIL was needless to say gutted, and refused to speak to her for three days on account of her gross insubordination. Sadly they kissed and made up in the cosy way that only these two paragons could, and we were back to normal.

There were times in the past when the Foghorn was muffled. In one of few mentions of the word LAVATORY she memorably collapsed in one. She also had a kind of nervous breakdown at one time. This was clearly induced by having to re-enact the feeding of the five thousand on an hourly basis.

Notwithstanding any health problems in the past, Foghorn has become super-human and the older she gets the more she takes on her shoulders. She keeps bees and chickens, runs a bed-and-breakfast business, does child-minding for all and sundry, takes part in VILLAGE PRODUCTIONS, serves on any committee that is formed, and her cooking activities are ridiculous. Yet she becomes ever cosier. The Foghorn will only be shaken out of her perpetual state of cosiness when Dayveed eventually mistakes Phil for a rat and attacks him with a spade and when it is conclusively confirmed that DAMIEN is indeed the son of Beelzebub.

FOOTBALL Our national sport, yet it is barely mentioned in Ambridge apart from the occasional haphazard kick around in the village. A few years back EDDIE took his boys to see Aston Villa, but that's it. No one at the bars of THE CAT or THE BULL ever chat about the weekend results. The poor form of Aston Villa for much of the 1997/98 season went unnoticed, and there was no interest in their EUEFA Cup campaign. Although DR DEATH alludes to being 'mad on football' neither he nor anyone else commented on the results of key games in the 1998 World Cup.

FREDA FRY At any given time there has to be a jam and home produce Fascist who seeks to achieve village domination as the supreme producer of pickles, jams, cakes and vegetables. This role was filled for many years by PRU, with the occasional pretender to the title such as the late MARTHA WOODFORD. It seems that the baton has now passed to Freda. Since she is the microwave operative at THE BULL, she obviously has a flair for these things. Unencumbered by the burden of speech, Freda is able to devote all her energies to producing the most phallic marrows. Being married to BERT must be a miserable experience, having to listen to the old git's ramblings and poetry. There is no immediate prospect of Freda developing a character, but you never know.

GAY PRIDE Many national events go unnoticed in Ambridge but one that certainly did not was the annual gay Pride March. This event, in which homosexuals get together in London, was the talk of the village in 1997 for about ten days before it occurred. Obviously the reason for its prominence was that SEAN completely abandoned the CRICKET team of which he was captain in order to go to this great festival. With the exception of SID PERKS, the whole village was entirely understanding and supportive. The likes of THE DOG WOMAN were to be heard saying, 'He's going to Pride you know' as if it was a meeting of the over-60s. The late but highly heterosexual JAAARN took it in his stride as if he expected the whole village to take a coach to Hyde Park. Apart from DIWALI it is now the most important date in the calendar of rural Borsetshire.

GEOFF TRAVIS Husband of MO and only a very occasional speaker. The single thing we ever heard about him was that he had a tendency to get 'very angry' if people chased him to pay his bills. Indeed it appeared that this got him a lot more angry than his wife trying to run off with one of his feed suppliers. To give him his due, when NEIL and JAILBIRD CARTER went round to his farm to confront Mo, he was pretty helpful and said that there would be no more trouble from her. Geoff was obviously going to give her the same treatment as his creditors. We suspect she now forms an integral part of Geoff's animal feed; as far as we are aware Neil long ceased selling feed to him.

GEORGE (ALCOPOP) BARFORD George is Yorkshire's answer to THE ONE-EYED MONSTER. He is forever whinging about something or other and has a chip on his shoulder that would take a baking potato to fashion. His main claim to fame, apart from liking the odd glass or 20, is that he murdered Patch, the beloved mutt of the now departed and forgotten ROBIN STOKES, who was once the unpaid vicar of Ambridge. Needless to say he was never reported for laying poison traps using prohibited chemicals.

George plays the cornet and chairs the parish Politburo. In 1997 he was assaulted for trying to impede the progress of some honest country folk who were, on a totally voluntary basis, culling some of JECK WOOLLEY's deer. He made something of a palaver over this event, took absolutely ages off work and, in order to assist his malingering, developed some sort of designer form of agoraphobia.

Now married to BORING CHRISTINE, Barford (a former policeman) deserted his Yorkshire wife Ellen and their two children, Terry and Karen, with the result that Terry went off the rails and turned to crime. He has basically taken over the role previously given to WALTER GABRIEL of making a rather silly and disapproving 'doh' noise every other sentence.

GINGER SPICE The calf lovingly reared by arsonist WIWYERM GRUNDY until it was manslaughtered by layabout father EDDIE who failed to clear up a whole host of ring pulls and other scrap metal from his fields. Cows are pretty stupid and don't seem to be able to taste the difference between a succulent mouthful of grass and half a drink can – until it's too late. THE VILLAGE BICYCLE kindly replaced Ginger Spice with Posh Spice: a Jersey heifer. Since it is apparently still alive, we can only presume Posh Spice is more partial to a ring-pull pasty. The idea that you might get David Beckham turning up and leaving the gate open is enough to make you think seriously about turning the beast into quality leather goods at the earliest opportunity.

GRACE ARCHER One of the establishment icons, Grace was a silly empty-headed woman who, had she lived, would have condemned herself to a life of jam making and servile subjugation to good old reliable PHIL. Made of poor-quality flammable material in an era prior to EU directives on such matters, Grace went up in smoke, which was highly inconsiderate since she was supposed to be at a dinner party at the time. The real tragedy about her demise back in the 1950s was that a load of sad listeners sent flowers to the BBC. These people now have worthy alternative activities available in the 1990s, such as anorak wearing, joining the dreaded Archers Addicts, or queuing overnight for the January sales. Phil used to comment on the anniversary of her death and even the FOGHORN would respectfully lower the decibel level of her voice to deafening. But we don't seem to observe the occasion nowadays.

GRAHAM RYDER We are clearly not intended to like Graham. He was brought in by HARDWORKING SIMON to manage the Estate when it became clear that the dreadful SHULA was making such a Horlicks of it, acting in a thoroughly unprofessional manner and letting her personal feelings get in the way of work. Graham, on the other hand, is cheerful and efficient.

At the Estate office Christmas party in 1996, while Shula was looking like a wet weekend, Graham was the life and soul with a string of tasteless jokes. This went down well with Hardworking Simon who likes to let his hair down on these occasions. The fact that the Estate has been sold and partially broken up does not seem to bother Graham who still seems to be managing it. He continues as one of BRIAN ALDRIDGE's henchman and plays a kind of Goebbels role. Graham has seemed very keen to get on the business side of THE VILLAGE BICYCLE's aristocratic knickers, but the spring seems to be going out of her mattress. One does begin to wonder about the bloke when he persuades a very reluctant Bicycle to go to a posh eight-star hotel in the Lake District, only to tell her when they get there how he doesn't fancy her. Graham is obviously completely screwed up and doesn't know whether he's best going for her, her horse or just maintaining a casual relationship with a flock of sheep. A great friend of PHALLUSTAIR BLANDVOICE, this relationship is presumably maintained, in large measure, to ensure a constant supply of animals.

GREG TURNER The keeper employed by BRIAN ALDRIDGE arrived in what was, for Ambridge, a most unusual manner. He was recruited for the job, his impending arrival was heralded and when he turned up he was introduced to people and spoke. This must have caused a whole host of petty jealousies in the village amongst those who thought he should have served his time before being allowed to speak. It seems de rigeur for keepers to be miserable sods with major attitude problems and Greg certainly fits the bill. He also fits in well with the essential role of any employee at Home Farm which is to resent DEBBIE and more or less ignore anything she asks to be done.

On his first day, Greg was accosted by poacher's son and arsonist WIWYERM GRUNDY who had been sent by FAT CLARRIE to 'introduce' himself. Dense Debbie failed to understand that Greg wanted to settle in and that welcoming Wiwyerm was about as sensible as inviting a fox to a hen-house. Greg made a great start by going to Brian for 'arbitration' the very first time he was asked by Debbie to do something with which he disagreed, and good old Brian backed up his professional keeper over the university drop-out. It may be early days, but Greg seems the sort of chap who will fit in just dandy.

GREY GABLES There are some very sinister aspects to Grey Gables, which tends to emulate the Bates Motel rather than a large country-house hotel, with country park, health club and golf course. One mystery is that it has virtually no staff although this is rarely a problem since it never really seems to have any guests either – even when it is full. It is rare for an unknown face to venture into the village shop but you might expect a fair number of guests to pop by. Occasionally even the riffraff of the village save up their emus and go for a meal at Grey Gables, but as with all other such establishments they only ever bump into other villagers. None of the locals ever play golf, leading us to believe some of the bunkers have probably been constructed to incorporate generous numbers of THE DISAPPEARED. JECK and PEGGOI are not getting any younger and it will be interesting to see what happens to the place in due course. Anarchists would love to see the return of HARDWORKING SIMON as proprietor – just imagine THE VILLAGE BICYCLE's reaction! But a more likely bet would be for Matt Crawford to get hold of it – the country park and golf course should be good for several thousand houses.

GUY PEMBERTON He was one of a whole string of fat cats to buy the Estate, taking up where Cameron Fraser had left off. Quite a nice bloke, he was unquestionably a kindly soul but Anarchists always took the view that he was too boring to live. THE VILLAGE BICYCLE was very quickly interested in the copious amounts of wonga he had about him. This was the beginning of his downfall. As a businessman, Guy instinctively realized that he ought to let his son, HARDWORKING SIMON, make the decisions regarding the Estate, but sadly he let his dick do the talking.

Once they were married, The Bicycle immediately established a regime of non-stop nagging, consistently trying to get the poor bloke to haul Simon over the coals. The final denouement came when she was bawling out Guy over the phone in order to make him poke his nose into the HARRIET WILLIAMS business. He finally croaked it with a massive heart attack. Had Ambridge had a proper doctor instead of DR DEATH, this would have been put down as manslaughter, and Caroline would have gone the way of JAILBIRD CARTER for a while. Instead she pocketed the Dower House and half a pub with a 'thank you very much'. The next businessman to enter the village should be on his mettle.

HANDBAG HEBDEN The only party political politician ever to have appeared in the village, Handbag Hebden was universally acknowledged as one of the most boring characters ever to run into a horse. Even SHULA (and this really is saying something) almost gave him the elbow because he was such a drip. Only his fat-cat lawyer's salary made her see monetary sense. Anyone else but Shula would have seen the danger signs: a bloke who was a Councillor for the SDP and had a mother called Bunty was bound to be pretty dire. As memory of him fast fades, there is little to recall of him: he liked CRICKET, he brought the first ethnic minority into the village (USHA), and he left a test tube of sperm with which to enable the construction of DAMIEN.

HARDWORKING SIMON Several Anarchists threatened to stop listening the day Hardworking Simon Pemberton was finally driven from the village. Never in the history of Ambridge has a man been so wronged. Already running a thriving business in Leamington, with his insatiable capacity for hard work he thought nothing of taking on the running of the Estate. It was inevitable that Simon's efficiency would cause problems for him, given that the Estate had been run by SHULA as a kind of family social club. Simon was keen to change the atmosphere in the Estate office so that it ceased to be a drop-in centre for JAILBIRD CARTER and Shula's endless number of friends and relations.

Simon had tried to befriend Shula, but we know how she reacted in the SLAP incident. His father, the goody-goody but harmless GUY PEMBERTON, had never given him the support he deserved, and once poor Guy fell into the avaricious clutches of THE VILLAGE BICYCLE, Simon was never going to succeed in Ambridge. The whole establishment turned against him when he tried to change the role of Grange Farm from scrap metal yard to that of a proper working farm with a decent crop of FLAX. The hypocrisy of the villagers was such that all the people who had spent years moaning about the Grundys were lining up to defend them when Simon tried to do something about them.

Shrewd businessman though he was, Simon made the mistake of giving some of the farming to DAYVEED and the ramshackle Brookfield operation. This caused him nothing but hassle and he was all set to take the work away from him. The big problem that he found was that none of the people he tried to do business with could separate their business lives from their personal lives. The straw that broke the camel's back was when DEBBIE ALDRIDGE, who had happily been playing hide the sausage with him, suddenly tried to blame him when she had a RIDING ACCIDENT. His defence lawyers attributed the whole business to OVERENTHUSIASM.

Always prepared to take the rap, Simon was a complete gentleman in court and Debbie was not even forced to give her perjured evidence. He did permit himself a well-deserved smile as he left the court, because he knew he was now off to Saudi Arabia for a good long time. We like to think he went off with HARRIET WILLIAMS, the only woman who really cared for him.

HARRIET WILLIAMS One of the most influential characters never to speak, Harriet was an old flame of HARD-WORKING. When her marriage hit a rocky patch, Simon kindly paid his respects to her. As far as we know, this did not include any OVERENTHUSIASM. A slight problem arose when Harriet kept phoning him at the Estate office and it transpired that this liaison was running concurrently with his rather misguided wooing of the dreaded SHULA.

THE VILLAGE BICYCLE blabbed to both Shula and GUY and indeed used her knowledge of this little matter to murder Guy in due course. For no apparent reason, calls from Harriet ceased soon after that SLAP – which was rather odd since the way should have been clear for her with Shula out of the picture. Harriet turned up at Guy's funeral following his murder, and of course this went down like Gerry Adams at an Orange Lodge with Shula and The Bicycle. It would be nice to think that she and Simon managed to get together in Saudi where Simon was heading after his minor court appearance. Hopefully she was able to give him the love and affection which had eluded him for so long and eventually they can live happily ever after in Leamington.

HARRY ROBERTS Harry works his butt off at Brookfield and gets no thanks whatsoever. He never arrived but is always there. He is mentioned once in a blue moon. Whining ROOOTH moaned that the poor bloke had had the nerve to book himself a week's holiday at Christmas 1997. He dare not speak but he's the unsung hero of the farm, toiling whilst others whinge.

HAY FEVER Despite the increase in asthma and pollen-related allergies often induced by modern crops such as rape, Ambridge has only managed to increase the number of sufferers in its midst from none to one. LYNDA SNELL, because she is an outsider from Sunningdale, dutifully suffers in true Forsterian fashion during the season, whenever she can remember. This doesn't seem to stop her from keeping a large number of pet animals. Happily she often seems to forget her allergy and it is quite normal to hear her uncongested tones at the height of the hay fever season. In 1998 it was suddenly mentioned that she was having hay fever injections, the total success of which will come as a great surprise to most people who have resorted to the same remedy.

HAYLEY JORDAN Those who have listened for a few years will remember that a girl called Julie worked at THE BULL for a while in the early 1980s. The similarities between her and Hayley are quite striking. Both were tarty Birmingham girls with Brum accents. Both reacted initially to life in Ambridge as if they had landed on the moon. Both made a beeline for pig farmers, (Julie for NEIL, Hayley for JAAARN) and then proceeded to moan that they were only interested in their pigs and that pigs smelt etc. And both entered into totally unsuitable arrangements with their chosen blokes.

One of the most distasteful features of Hayley in this PC world is that she is overtly sexist and treated Jaaarn as a sex object. She was forever referring to 'his cute little bum' (when children might be listening – no wonder young people are in the state they are), and making sexual innuendo. It was quite understandable that he sought solace in the true love of SHARON – someone who wanted him for his wallet as well as his body.

Hayley is as tactful as an atomic bomb and is frequently putting her foot in it – a particularly memorable occasion being when she 'inadvertently' told ROY TUGGER about KATE's pregnancy. The night before Jaaarn went FERGIE racing, he took Hayley to THE MONT BLANC where he proposed to her. She turned him down flat, and of course the moment he turned up his toes she was sobbing all over the shop and telling everyone how much she loved him.

The irrationality with which Hayley decided that she wanted to take over Jaaarn's pig business, despite living with her Mum in Birmingham and not having had any agricultural training, indicates that she really should have been sectioned under the Mental Health Act. It is particularly unsafe for the lovely Sharon Richards to walk the streets while Hayley is on the loose since Hayley believes that only she is entitled to any claims on Jaaarn's memory. Anarchists strongly suspect that by the time people are reading this book she will have married the pedestrian ROY TUGGER, Ambridge's own Gabriel Oak.

HAZEL WOOLLEY Why, oh why can we not have a return to Ambridge for the lovely Hazel? She always caused mayhem whenever she came to the village – particularly upsetting THE VILLAGE BICYCLE, which can't be a bad thing. Hazel would really get up PEGGOI's nose, and although she is only the step-daughter of JECK, it is rather odd that she *never* turns up now. So far as we know Jeck is about the only family she has, as her mother Valerie Woolley is now pushing up the daisies. To many listeners, Hazel is just a name, but to the die-hards she is the thinking man's SHARON.

HEYDON BERROW This is another of the places that people are often 'over at/in' – just like MARNEYS or LAKEY HILL. We envisage it as the local rubbish tip, a place where the methane is building nicely towards a spectacular display of pyrotechnics on the day of Armageddon.

HIGGS JECK WOOLLEY's chauffeur and chrysanthemum grower. John Higgs is one of those characters who people will often claim have never spoken. This is not true, as he has uttered several words from time to time, and has emitted some particu-larly fine grunts over the years. On one occasion he was drunk as a skunk and was highly audible. Apart from LYNDA, THE VILLAGE BICYCLE, and JEAN-PAUL, no one at GREY GABLES has much to say, so he is only par for the golf course.

HORNY HUGH A 'business friend' of ELIZABETH PARGETTER's who was/is hung like a horse. Elizabeth was disap-pearing for weeks on end to run 'courses' for him, leaving drippy NIGEL to hold the fort at LOWER LOXLEY. We were in no doubt that this was cover for the fact that hide the sausage was being played in a big way. The biggest give away was that Elizabeth had only been in business at Lower Loxley for five minutes and was clearly struggling to market her own enterprise. On the basis that 'those who can't, teach', it may have been just about plausible but we all sympathized when Nigel objected to her absences. Nigel may be stupid, but even he smelt a rat when, one weekend, Elizabeth announced that Horny Hugh had turned up unexpectedly in the area and that she would therefore have to entertain him. After all we are talking about a bloke from London who is a mere 90 miles or so from home, not an American tourist. Horny was putting good money her way, but everyone realized that this was the launch of her career as a hooker rather than as a John Harvey-Jonesette.

HOWARD FRIEND Howard was an interesting character whose allegedly malign influence has disappeared without trace or comment. He came on the scene to oppose TONY and PAT's attempts to enlarge their farm shop. On the face of it this was due to environmental reasons but Tony's millimetre-long fuse soon blew when it transpired that the bloke was intending to open his own organic shop. Tony is the Wall Street of the organic vegetable retailing world and when he sneezes THE ONE-EYED MONSTER catches a cold. In a small area it would have been reasonable to assume that a second organic retail outlet would pose a threat to Tony and then Mike, but we have never heard another word about it. Did the shop open? What happened?

HUNTING AND THE COUNTRYSIDE Ambridge folk have a big problem with hunting. As a rural village steeped in tradition with plenty of obvious candidates as hunting enthusiasts, we ought to hear a considerably greater amount of pro-hunting talk and coverage of meets than we do of sidelines such as the dreaded VILLAGE PRODUCTIONS. Yet we don't. There are very occasional fleeting references to it, for example DEBBIE may be apologetically described as having 'gone to the meet'. PHALLUSTAIR and one or two others are self-confessed hunters but there are no hounds in the village. There was a very brief reference to a couple of people (THE VILLAGE BICYCLE and BORING CHRISTINE) having gone to the 1997 Countryside Rally at Hyde Park, with marginally more people showing a vague interest in the 1998 march. Boring Christine, SHULA, The Bicycle and Debbie all hunt, but because they live in such a PC village they are clearly scared to mention it. So a ban on hunting would doubtless go unchallenged in Ambridge. No one would lose their jobs, and no one would care.

ILLNESS Ambridge is a very healthy place. It is extremely rare for someone to have a serious illness that hospitalizes them, although the mistaken hospitalization of DAMIEN, who really only needed exorcizing, is something of an exception. The only reason they go to hospital is because of an accident or to give birth (sometimes one follows the other). But it is most rare for someone to become ill and need an operation. If anyone is ill they simply die – like poor MARTHA.

IPPY The Shergar of Ambridge. He was THE VILLAGE BICYCLE's horse that completely DISAPPEARED and was never found. The facts are that she neglected him, and he got fed up standing in a field waiting to be turned into Copydex, so one day he leapt the fence and found somewhere better to live. Who can honestly blame him?

JAAARN ARCHER The unexpected demise of Jaaarn rocked the nation in February 1998. Anarchists genuinely regretted his death, principally because if anyone was to be crushed to death by a tractor there were plenty of eminently more deserving candidates. In contrast to his cousin DAYVEED, Jaaarn had an enviable degree of hedonism about him. He was hardly out of short trousers before he was bringing credence to the wise old saying 'Never come a knockin' when the caravan's a rockin''. When the lovely SHARON was staying in a grace and favour caravan on his parents' farm, we were delighted to see them strike up such an ideal partnership. It got up PAT's nose considerably since she is a hypocrite of the worst order. Jaaarn lavished fatherly concern on KYLIE and when SHARON managed to get a council house in the village, Jaaarn moved in with her. When she dumped him he was understandably a bit miffed but quickly recovered and established himself as the local stud, putting it about left right and centre.

By setting himself up in the disco business he had wisely twigged that DJs tend to have more groupies than pig farmers, something that NEIL CARTER has never really understood. He was quite money orientated, and why not? Thanks to numerous successful entrepreneurial ventures he had amassed plenty of chick-pulling dosh, which certainly came in handy while he was bankrolling Sharon and Kylie during their sojourn in the village. The coupling between Jaaarn and the dreadful HAYLEY has always been somewhat irritating and it was fitting that it should be Sharon who managed to end it.

Jaaarn died amid a welter of CASTISM where the BBC and Archers Anoraks really excelled themselves in trying to destroy our vivid picture of Ambridge life. Pictures of some spotty actor were mysteriously appearing in newspapers throughout the land, always attached to some ridiculous story about poor old Jaaarn. A former and repeated winner of the SINGLE WICKET TROPHY, Jaaarn's memory will live on through his pork.

JAILBIRD CARTER Susan is desperate to climb out of her underclass. Born into the noble family of Horrobin, she was wooed by NEIL CARTER and a shotgun wedding ensued. Her big class-climbing break came when she was given a job in the Estate office. Working under the slack and sloppy supervision of the appalling SHULA, life there was one long holiday. She was forever on the phone to her mates, at the Estate's expense, and HARDWORKING SIMON in particular found it highly irritating when people would call in to the office willy nilly to discuss WI and other non-work-related matters. When Jailbird was finally given the heave-ho from the Estate, they must have noticed an immediate reduction in the photocopying bill as she was constantly stealing large runs to produce leaflets for the dreaded VILLAGE PRODUCTIONS, and the endless number of do-gooding meetings she attends.

A delightful episode occurred when her ambitious brother CLIVE, a credit to the Horrobin name, decided to visit her and give himself a little break from prison – all part of the gradual rehabilitation programme so necessary if he was to play his full part in the community. Jailbird perverted the course of justice by sheltering him in a kack-handed and obvious way. She was rightly sent to prison, and showed just what a recidivist she is by absconding to attend the funeral of old HANDBAG HEBDEN. The typical hypocrisy of the village came into its own at this point. On the one hand there was Clive who had left prison without permission, and everyone was saying that 'hanging would be too good for him, throw away the key', etc. But when Jailbird did precisely the same thing, the whole village was up in arms about how unfair it was that she should be given an extra ten days for her rank disobedience.

Like many Ambridge mothers, Jailbird has a rather dubious parental record. Her daughter EMMA was a serial bedwetter, largely on account of having a mother whose idea of fashion was a trouser suit with an attractive arrow pattern on it. When Christopher was born, she turned against him simply because he looked like the elephant man and had 666 tattooed on his trunk. It simply didn't fit into her plan to have a child that could not be used as a model for Mothercare.

Jailbird has always been something of a Vicar of Bray, and was changing sides more times than a 78 record over the Pemberton v Grundy issue. At first, when it looked as if Pemberton would win hands down, and her so-called 'mates' the Grundys would be living in cardboard boxes, she was careful to keep quiet about his plans to evict them. FAT CLARRIE refused to speak to her when she realized that Jailbird had temporarily acted like a loyal employee and remained stum over the FLAX plans. But when it was quite obvious that everyone had deserted poor HARD-WORKING SIMON, she was all too ready to stab him in the back along with everyone else by betraying his confidence and sending information to the tribunal. Amusingly, with Simon gone, and the business units underway, Jailbird thought that she would be made the manager. After all, she *had* photocopied a few sheets of paper relating to the plans and she therefore regarded herself as an expert. Anarchists went wild with joy when BRIAN summoned her to tell her that he was indeed able to offer her a new job – as cleaner. Typically she went round saying how he could stick his job, and then proceeded to accept it.

Another class-climbing opportunity presented itself early in 1998 as she signed up as receptionist to DR DEATH. At the surgery she is in her element, throwing her weight about and trying to prevent deserving patients from visiting the quack.

When Neil chucked in his job, Jailbird was typically unsympathetic – so determined was she that he should be a sales rep, regardless of how miserable it made him. She was forced to go cap in hand to Brian to ask for her cleaning job back but Brian was able to tell her that he had now reallocated the job to someone who really appreciated it. Her return to the village shop is deplorable especially as JECK, who was so keen to hold interviews, still ended up employing someone with a criminal record. The sooner Jailbird returns to her rightful place doing a long stretch in the nick, the better for us all.

JEAN-PAUL An entirely incredible character, he is nothing more than a French voice with a camp, prima donna-ish dose of stereotyping. We all realize that it is impossible to cook unless you are French, but he really is too ridiculous a character to exist outside of a pantomime. Despite the fact that GREY GABLES sometimes seems quite large, there is never any mention of any other cooking staff or relief chefs, so Jean-Paul must work damn hard. We go a long time without hearing him, presumably because he's always in the kitchen and we're not.

JECK WOOLLEY A star amongst men. Jeck Woolley, born in Stirchley, is a typical self-made man. He has no subtlety but his trademark pomposity has greatly subsided with age. Jeck really has undergone a fair degree of repackaging over the years and we can only assume that a top advertising agency has got hold of him. At one time, he wanted to be guest of honour at every event, chairman of every committee, etc. But now he is more like Uriah Heep in his general humility.

Jeck is not short of a bob or two and owns GREY GABLES country park, the *Borchester Echo* and the village shop. We greatly enjoy his tendency to interfere with the management of his enterprises, such as his insistence on introducing the 'Pleasant Valley' products into the shop. Even at his great age, Jeck was keen to introduce an equal opportunities policy when he needed a part-time assistant. This was presumably in case USHA or SEAN were a bit short of the readies.

The most interesting feature of Jeck is the strange noises he makes when he hears some bad news or has his feelings hurt. When he speaks he has some amazing inflexions. It would seem that when the good Lord was dishing out adenoids, Jeck was occupying the first three places in the queue, which goes a long way to explaining why he calls THE VILLAGE BICYCLE 'Carolide'. For anyone with a dodgy ticker, Jeck is something of an icon as he seemed to have his first heart attack aged about two, and to have survived on a diet of lard ever since. He's going to be in his 80s soon and is one of the few people who, when he pops his clogs, will be mourned by Anarchists throughout the land.

JIM COVERDALE Something that people have to realize about the PC village of Ambridge is that all police nowadays are Fascists. This was not always the case. Some years back PC Colin Drury was quite popular with the likes of DAN, but probably because he turned a blind eye to Dan's more dubious activities. Since then it's been downhill all the way. Coverdale was detested as the local bobby, and he then went off and married the Aldridge au pair Eva Lenz into whose knickers quite a large number of the village populace had sought to get (notably NEIL CARTER). Then last year, Coverdale returned for no apparent reason as a Detective Inspector. Laudably he was trying to get EDDIE banged up for duffing up GEORGE (ALCOPOP) BARFORD, but even Jim was no match for the Ambridge mafia. The strange thing is that apart from Eddie, no one seemed at all surprised at Coverdale's return, nor showed any interest in it. Not one person asked after Eva who had been quite a well-known figure in the village. Not even one of the Aldridges remarked on the subject.

JOAN PARGETTER If you are going to change your name, you might as well make it a substantial change like, for example, from Tracy to Heavenly Hirani Tiger Lily. NIGEL's mum changed hers from Joan to Julia, yet the revelation that she had done this still shook the village to its roots. Joan is an easy person to be, as she is an actress. She sounds like an actress and is generally quite an incredible character. She has been dealt a very poor deal by both her son and daughter-in-law. If you think that LOWER LOXLEY was her marital home for years, it is quite outrageous that they should have kicked her out and, on the rare occasions that she is allowed there, should make it so unpleasant for her. Hardly surprising then that she sought solace in the bottle.

Joan is no fool and detested ELIZABETH whom she rightly regarded as a common farmer's daughter and well below the station of her Nigel. She joined with Anarchists in deriding their highly unnatural treatment of ELLIE MAY. She wrongly felt that DEBBIE would have made a better wife for Nigel, for as we know, Debbie will always be one of life's bridesmaids.

Joan has enjoyed a rather curious friendship with NELSON over recent years, and it is rather sad that as she seeks comfort and refuge from her unfriendly family, the best she can do is an old queen with a background of armed robbery and antiques fraud. Her best bet might be to see a good solicitor to find out whether or not she may have a case for turfing Nigel and Elizabeth out of Lower Loxley.

JOE GRUNDY Anarchists respect Joe. He knows that the cosy establishment will never offer him the genuine hand of friendship and he retains a healthy outlook on life in Ambridge. As he sees it, the whole village has to run for the benefit of the Archer clan. If anyone else has a problem, it will only be solved if it is also a problem for an Archer. It was typical of the kind of thing that gets up our noses that when they were thinking of a soppy name for the DAN ARCHER NUCLEAR TESTING SITE, no one would countenance naming it after Joe's late wife Susan. The lazy git that he is, Joe has traded on chronic farmer's lung, though it is more likely to be farmer's liver as he regularly gets boozed up, preferably at someone else's expense. Over the years, the establishment has become more accepting of the Grundys, which tends to make us feel less empathy with them. He has an extremely unlikely tendency to seek to defraud his own family, including his grandchildren. If he lived in London's East End he would have been the recipient of a concrete overcoat long ago.

JOLYON GIBSON This public-school-educated junkie, shacked up with KATE, bonked her contemporaneously with her relationship with ROY and introduced a fine crop of cannabis plants to the village. Sadly he was arrested for his green-fingered endeavours and we have never heard of him since. An all-round good guy, who would make an excellent husband to SHULA.

JULIAN GOODACRE (BAGPIPEMAKER) A regular and much-valued correspondent to the Archers Anarchist newsletter, one of the finest makers of bagpipes in the land, and a keen detestor of SHULA. If you have bagpipes to buy, then buy them from this man.

KATE ALDRIDGE MRS HIGH AND MIGHTY's third child by a third bloke. Like her mother before her, Kate became pregnant at an early age by a father who would not be regarded by her own parents as a 'good catch'. Luther, a Caribbean Swampy, was a bit much for Ambridge under the mildest of circumstances, but for him to sire what could ultimately be the heir to Home Farm was not quite in BRIAN ALDRIDGE's marketing plan.

Kate is one of the Ambridge brats who has been unstintingly obnoxious from birth. Her obsession with being alternative and green follows in the same well-sandalled footprints as LUCY PERKS and ELIZABETH PARGETTER, although Kate is perhaps taking longer to grow out of it. A couple of years back we all had a good laugh when she disappeared with a bunch of 'travellers' who were busy alternativing themselves all over the UK. When Brian had to identify a body found beneath some Cornish cliff we were agog. So what a non-CLIFF-HANGER it turned out to be when it wasn't Kate. The episode ended with Brian turning up to look at the body and the next evening opened with someone like FOGHORN talking about the price of eggs and casually mentioning what a relief it had been that the body hadn't been Kate's.

Like mother, like daughter, Kate is totally spoilt and even Brian, who sees right through her, doesn't seem to put his foot down. Kate lives rent free in one of the holiday cottages, scrounges food from her mother, and holds down no job for more than five minutes before getting bored with it or being fired. And the way Kate treated ROY TUGGER is nothing short of criminal. He has lavished love and affection on her in the manner only a village idiot can. In return, Kate has treated him like a bucket of the proverbial. The PC birth of Winstona in a muddy bender at the Glastonbury Festival, aided by Morwena the wicked witch, will doubtless lead to a spate of copycat births throughout the country. No grubby wigwam can be considered safe. Pleasingly, both Brian and Mrs High and Mighty are so right-on that they did not even comment on the colour of their first grandchild. But if the deranged Roy continues to claim the child is his, we will know that he has finally flipped.

KATHY PERKS One of Ambridge's most irritating whingers, and that really is saying something. We first heard of her when she was called Miss Holland and was LUCY PERKS' domestic-science teacher at school. It later emerged that she was a fraud on two counts. First, she was still married at the time, and should therefore have been *Mrs*. Second, one might have been forgiven for thinking that a domestic-science teacher should be an able and willing cook, if they expect to have a career telling other people how to do it. The opportunity to own and run a restaurant should therefore be manna from heaven. Yet this woman, ever since she married SID PERKS, has had to be dragged kicking and screaming into the kitchen.

Kathy got together with Sid when he rented her Rose Cottage – a little bolt hole he had bought for himself and his first wife, the late POLL DOLL. Eventually, after a fair bit of playing hard to get, and some two-timing with the then local bobby DAVE BARRY, Kathy married Sid and has proceeded to make his life a misery ever since. What Sid has always needed to make THE BULL a success is to be in a proper partnership, but the dreaded Kathy kept going on about wanting her own career, space, all the usual stuff. Kathy finally gave up her teaching job, but instead of helping Sid she went off to GREY GABLES and effectively worked in competition with him, just as former Bull cook, THE VILLAGE BICYCLE, had done before her. In order to mess up Sid's life even further, she went AWOL with DS Barry. Sid had the good sense to show her the door but the rather less good sense to un-show it somewhat later.

Things have never really improved. They had the sprog Jamie, a child about whom we should clearly be concerned due to his constant neglect. But Kathy has just continued moaning endlessly about her role in life. She was all keen about setting up the restaurant venture when they eventually bought the pub from PEGGOI WOOLLEY with dear old GUY PEMBERTON but she seems to think it can run itself without her getting her hands dirty. Kathy often talks as if she is the great intellectual force behind the business, and clearly feels that cooking is beneath her. Yet the marketing and creative side of The Bull appears to be the very thing that is letting it down.

Christmas 1997 was really the last straw; after a disastrous year for The Bull in which all the heterophobic villagers preferred going to THE CAT which isn't even in the village, Sid finally thought he had scored one over on The Cat when he had a completely full restaurant on Christmas Day. But was Kathy pleased? No, she spent the day saying how it had completely ruined Jamie's Christmas, and how she was never going to cook on Christmas Day again. She might reflect that if she'd opted for DS Barry, or an ambulance man, water-board official, vicar, or even farmer, Jamie would have found a similarly disrupted Christmas, but would doubtless have survived.

KENTON ARCHER An odious smarm ball of the worst order. As the twin of the dreaded SHULA what can one expect? Kenton is a crook and a waster. The mystery is how he has come by any money at all since he is transparently stupid despite his endless posing. He is a kind of middle-class ONE-EYED MONSTER in that nothing he throws himself into seems to succeed for long. The good thing is that he disappears to

Australia for long periods of time, and we don't have to hear him. He is usually on the 'apologies for absence' spot at family gatherings, but Christmas 1997 saw a particularly indigestible dose of him. He managed to get under the skin of ROOOTH and DAYVEED by showering large presents on the awful PEEEP. In fact, it was hard to see what their problem was with this since they bestow precious little attention on Peep and her brother BSE Josh themselves.

Anarchists have long been of the opinion that Kenton may be something of a SEAN, though he did go on about someone called Mel back in Oz who was apparently 25 and had long blond hair. Had he realized how homosexual Ambridge now is, he could have brought rent-boy Melvin with him. Kenton managed to persuade Shula that they should both celebrate their impending 40th birthdays at New Year. There then followed the most absurd situation imaginable where the venue was NELSON's wine bar, and where ELIZABETH had quite amazingly handed over complete control of the place to Kenton. This despite her having been entrusted by Nelson to run the bar in his absence. Kenton didn't bother with proper invitations and allowed all the normal customers at the wine bar to enjoy free drinks all night. During his visit, it emerged that he was allegedly married to this Mel person – for reasons of tax. Most parents would have been quite taken aback by this news and, to give him his due, PHIL was not exactly dancing for joy. FOGHORN reacted with the immortal words, 'Better get that pie out of the oven.' If we were to believe Kenton (and why on earth should we?) he was in big trouble this time with the tax man. He will never learn his lesson of course because dopey Phil promptly shelled out a few grand to keep him going whilst sanctimonious Shula paid all his Ambridge debts for him.

KYLIE RICHARDS The beautiful damsel begat of CLIVE and his good lady SHARON. Her name betrays the prejudices of those who think that Sharon is thick and that only thick people name their children after people in Australian soaps. Kylie was one of many non-speaking stalwarts in the village and one might have thought she would be a tearaway and delinquent when she reached her teens.

Despite being a young girl, she is always referred to as if she is a toddler. Some years back, Kylie beat ALICE in a vicious fancy-dress competition, much to the chagrin of MRS HIGH AND MIGHTY. Just before JAAARN turfed her and her mother out of his cottage, Kylie suddenly spoke, and revealed herself to be a thoroughly pleasant, articulate girl. Needless to say her accent was completely unlike her mother's and it is quite clear that Clive has funded her with a private education or perhaps a governess, not to mention regular elocution lessons.

LAKEY HILL A cross between Mount Olympus and Hampstead Heath, this is a place where people go when they are feeling down. Given the number of people who are perennially down in Ambridge it must be like Piccadilly Circus. No doubt littered with used condoms and syringes, it is also where SHULA and many others have been for a bit of Midlands nookie. The correct placing of these locations can be a bit tricky and can lead to some manifestations of the most crass CASTISM. If you care to read *The Book of the Archers*, you will see a description of Lakey Hill as being 'to the north east of Ambridge'. No problem there, but the inside cover has one of those ghastly castist creations – a map. And where is Lakey Hill shown? Slap bang in the south east. Something about arses and elbows comes to mind. But it does go to show that castists never prosper.

LANCASTRIAN TOMMY Strangely, despite being the progeny of Welsh PAT and Ambridge-born TONY, and not withstanding the fact that he had spent his entire mute childhood in the village, Tommy is a Lancastrian with a broad accent to prove it. He didn't find it necessary to speak until his GCSE results appeared in 1997. He then went from silent shrinking violet to ring leader of the most debauched and inebriate party ever seen beneath the hallowed beams of the village hall. Much to BORING CHRISTINE's chagrin, not only did he cause damage and excessive mess to the hall, but he treated the DUCKS on the VILLAGE POND to an unexpected supper of diced carrot. But that's the traditional Lancastrian way of letting your hair down.

Like his brother before him, Tommy had the hots for SHARON when she reappeared on the scene, but just as when

JAAARN was interested in her at the same tender age, the love went unrequited. He's only got to wait a few years and perhaps she'll be back for him. PAT would just love it. Since the sad death of Jaaarn, Lancastrian Tommy has, in many ways, taken up where he left off. He has developed a superficial interest in the memorial pigs and seems to be developing a difficult and cantankerous attitude. Quite rightly he will never forgive Jaaarn for messing up his birthday. There was Tommy dressed up to the nines and ready to party while Jaaarn, wallowing in self-pity, was more interested in doing wheelies on his FERGIE. His failure to win the SINGLE WICKET in the year of his brother's death brought shame on the Archer name and the whole of Lancashire. The bookies will give you only 7/4 against him marrying HAYLEY.

LAURELS, THE This is a secure establishment that houses FAT MAN FORREST, PRU and no one else. There is no evidence that it is a private home so we assume it is run by the council – which makes it extremely unlikely that it is the paradise we have been led to believe it is. We don't know its location but we have numerous candidates to send there when we find out.

LAVATORY With the very honourable exception of MR PULLEN whose whole *raison d'être* is going to the lavatory, and FOGHORN who many years ago collapsed in one, no one else ever goes. You never hear someone say 'Where's PHIL?' and Foghorn reply, 'Oh he's just popped to the loo.' Oh no, he's always 'over in MARNEYS'. Most of the characters have excellent waterworks although suddenly in one episode *both* BRAIN ALDRIDGE and MATT CRAWFORD 'popped to the bathroom', not at the same time we hasten to add.

LIBBY PURVES A great icon to Anarchists since she dared to write that, 'Someone had to SLAP SHULA.' On these grounds she was made a lifelong honorary member of our august body. She cannot do a thing wrong, however arty-farty and cosy her *Midweek* programme may be.

LILLIAN BELLAMY We like Lillian. She's one of those people who knows how to carry her wealth. Lillian oozes class. Unlike her sister MRS HIGH AND MIGHTY who is just rich, Lillian is absolutely rolling in the stuff. She lives in Guernsey, partly for tax reasons but mainly to get well away from her whinging family. If you remember that she inherited the Berrow Estate from her husband Ralph before the likes of CAMERON FRASER and HARDWORKING SIMON had got into breaking it up, you will realize just how seriously rich she is.

Lillian really enjoys a drink and when she comes to the village she is friendlier to the Grundys than to her own family. Her son James is one of THE DISAPPEARED which must be sad for her. Considering that it can't be a matter of saving up for the air fare her visits to Ambridge are rare indeed. But then, faced with the choice of a pint of SHIRES at the empty BULL or a few glasses of champers with Bergerac, there's really no contest.

LILY OF LAYTON CROSS, THE Jolene Rogers had shown a lot of promise and at one time EDDIE had been all set to walk up the aisle with her. She was another Borsetshire bicycle but without THE VILLAGE BICYCLE's class.

A wearer of fine leather and possessor of a voice like a nightingale, Jolene has pursued a country-and-western career which has been just marginally less unsuccessful than Eddie's. Sadly her relationship with Eddie never quite flourished and she went off with the unlikely named Mr Wayne Tucson, a fellow country-and-western artiste. This did not endure and there was a good opportunity for her to put a bit of lead back into Eddie's pencil when she showed up again a couple of years ago. But Jolene seems to have

undergone a moral transformation and was heard to tell FAT
CLARRIE that she had nothing to fear. More's the pity, Eddie is
much more entertaining when he is up to no good, and it is always
fun to hear Clarrie imitating an exploding monkfish.

LINE DANCING A sad pastime which in most parts of the
country tends to take place on a Wednesday afternoon, and so
presumably is patronized largely by librarians. In Ambridge, THE
LILY OF LAYTON CROSS introduced it as a night-time event at
THE BULL and it went down a storm with all the village anoraks.
Inevitably SID and KATHY managed to lose it to THE CAT on
the basis that any form of dancing so gormless that it just requires
you to stand in a line holding hands was going to appeal to SEAN
MYERSON's clientele. Now we rarely hear of it. You might have
thought that morris dancing would be more appropriate in a rural
English village, but that just wouldn't be PC enough for Ambridge.

LOONY LARRY LOVELL This weird man suddenly
appeared without warning as the self-appointed director of one
of the dreaded VILLAGE PRODUCTIONS. His taste in women
spans several ages as he has been pursuing both FOGHORN
(nearing 70) and THE VILLAGE BICYCLE. Larry has clearly been
planted by the BBC to make us think that *The Archers* is a soap
opera with parts played by actors. They should hang their heads
in shame – it's all part of the dumbing-down process.

LOWER LOXLEY The Pargetters turned NIGEL's ancestral
home into a two-bit conference centre. It has caused constant
friction between Nigel and ELIZABETH since Nigel appears
(against the odds for a complete idiot) to be doing most of the
work, while, for a great deal of the time, Elizabeth has been giving
HORNY HUGH one . It appears to be run in a chaotic fashion,
as a kind of Fawlty Towers. It is unknown where the money came

from to turn the place into a business because Nigel was always stony broke, and it is hard to imagine him convincing a bank manager to let him open an account, let alone borrow money.

We don't hear too much about the place because it is out of the village. There was a very nasty dose of quasi VILLAGE PRODUCTION in 1996 when Lower Loxley was used as a film set. All sorts of characters from the village got involved as 'extras' and the whole nightly episode was dominated with a complete summer pantomime for weeks on end. It was appalling, but it's over, and we can now sleep peacefully in our beds.

LUCY PERKS One of the many useless features of this book is the completely gratuitous and mind-bendingly uninteresting bits of information we give you. Did you know that the very first words that Lucy ever uttered were, 'My name is Lucy Perks, THE BULL, Ambridge'? If you think about it, it is a trifle unusual to attach your address to your name, especially when you have never spoken before. The good thing about Lucy was that she didn't like KATHY. She saw through her right from the start, and realized that she was no substitute for her mother, POLL DOLL.

Like most of the teenage girls in the village she became a green-tinged Lefty, sabotaging Brookfield's milking parlour and jumping aboard the animal-welfare bandwagon. She also helped out a ne'er-do-well centre in Borchester. Just the sort of thing that TFW would encourage nowadays. Lucy also twigged pretty quickly when Kathy was carrying on with DAVE BARRY. She had a very peculiar automaton's intonation when she first spoke, but then developed a very clear voice without the trace of a local accent despite her rural upbringing, and her father's Brum brogue. As soon as Lucy finished at university she went off to New Zealand and got married. She is now one of Ambridge's DISAPPEARED, although SID has been known to talk to a phone that allegedly has her at the other end of it.

LYNDA SNELL Anarchists like Lynda because most of the village establishment sneer at her behind her back, and sometimes to her face. If they don't like her, she must be a good thing. For older listeners, Lynda is a replacement for Aunt Laura in that she is wheeled out whenever any issue requires a campaign. It must be very frustrating for her that the PARISH COUNCIL is run by deadbeats such as GEORGE (ALCOPOP) BARFORD. The campaigns Lynda has led are too numerous and uninteresting to mention, but some of them have been very successful. For example, you *never* hear any TRAFFIC in the village since people lost interest in her campaign against it.

Ambridge has never lived up to the standards Lynda had come to expect from having lived in the civilized southern enclave of Sunningdale, and the shabby way she has been treated speaks volumes for the insular and unwelcoming nature of the village. It has been suggested that Lynda could be in league with the Devil – her propensity to keep goats does little to dispel this notion. We quite understand how humiliating it must be for her to have to work as a receptionist at GREY GABLES when her boss TRUDY PORTER never speaks to her, and THE VILLAGE BICYCLE treats her as if she is a naughty adolescent school girl. The one thing we do hate about Lynda is her insatiable desire for VILLAGE PRODUCTIONS. If another one were never to be staged for a million years that would be too soon.

LYNX Some years ago, an innocent lynx was roaming around the country park under the misapprehension that that is what country parks are there for, when JECK WOOLLEY, in a show of bravado, shot it dead. He then stuffed it, and put it in a glass case in GREY GABLES where it gazes down to this day. It used to be mentioned occasionally but nowadays only long in the tooth Anarchists are aware of its existence. If you remember the lynx, you'll want to take a look at SWEARING.

m

MANORFIELD CLOSE Ambridge's answer to Porton Down, a collection of homes for people who are born old but rather grotesquely never die. The main characteristic of the inhabitants is that they never speak and they are only referred to in terms of their incapacities: MR PULLEN (waterworks), MRS POTTER (walking frame), MRS BARRACLOUGH (cancer and then murdered).

MARNEYS Whenever you go to Brookfield to visit any of the farming folk, they are always 'over in Marneys'. We are left to conjecture what this means, although it seems to be a code for 'not in'. Whilst the establishment would like you to believe it is an ancient name for a field over yonder, unkind folk have suggested it is a shed containing a stack of tins of SHIRES and a large pile of dirty magazines.

MARTHA WOODFORD People have already forgotten about Martha. She was the village postmistress, cleaner of the telephone box and feeder of bread to the DUCKS. Martha was also a great gossip, and often spread stories that were largely untrue. For that we loved her.

People have always had problems with becoming senile in Ambridge, FAT MAN FORREST being a good example. Martha was a fine example of Saundersism: she went from being completely scatty to turning up at the PARISH COUNCIL and questioning technical points of planning law. Her demise was rather sad because, as so often happens in this self-centred village, everyone completely forgot about her, failed to visit her, or even to mention her, and then just announced she had died.

There is nothing so 'ex' as an ex *Archers*' character. But *we'll* always remember you Martha.

MATT CRAWFORD One of the main players in Borchester Land, Matt Crawford is a man who has the Midlands countryside coursing through his cockney veins. He is to the Ramblers Association what a beefburger is to a vegetarian. But he understands business and he likes to see profits. If he could turn Ambridge into a version of his beloved Old Kent Road he'd be in his seventh heaven and who are we to stop him?

MEMBER OF PARLIAMENT There doesn't seem to be one covering Ambridge. Although there are a few acknowledgements of the existence of elections, no MP ever visits the village. Perhaps more unusual is the fact that people like LYNDA SNELL never write to their MP. Strange when you think it is a particularly likely step to take in times of planning decisions such as the bypass and the threat of 12 new homes on Sawyers Farm. Yet they seem to get on quite happily without representation at Westminster. Perhaps this could be a model for the rest of us.

MEN'S PROBLEMS It is an unfair world, and men would have it no other way. But it should be mentioned that Ambridge is even less fair. Whereas 'women's things' do get the odd airing we hear very little of anything in the men's department. The only exception is that there was a strong inference that ROBIN STOKES suffered from being stuck at half-past six when he had to perform with THE VILLAGE BICYCLE. Otherwise, nothing to report, and the idea that an Ambridge man should require a prostate operation is clearly preposterous.

MILK TANKER Under the careful stewardship of Kevin, it drove into a car containing PAT and POLL DOLL (the late Mrs

Perks). Sadly it got the wrong person which meant not only that Pat is still with us but that the good SID ended up marrying the awful KATHY. In the days when the milk tanker was mentioned, good old Kevin often got a mention alongside it. Strangely no one ever stopped to ask what effect the whole dreadful business had on poor Kevin. It is typical of Ambridge folk never to look beyond their own village.

MILLENNIUM Like many villages, Ambridge is doing its unnecessary bit for this arbitrary festival – planting a load of trees. Wow, that's so exciting, you can just feel THE ONE-EYED MONSTER's logger beginning to twitch. Predictably the tree-planting project is being presided over by the usual sanctimonious suspects, THAT FISHER WOMAN and SHULA are never far away from such action. The thing to look out for as we approach the big day is an example of incongruous Mandelsonian PRODUCT PLACEMENT. We understand that the government is desperate to promote the dreary Dome by encouraging the organization of coach parties from Ambridge, Coronation Street, Brookside Close, and other well-known locations, to visit it. Quite how ridiculous this would be remains to be seen since it largely depends on the eventual enthusiasm for the thing nearer the time. But, as with other SUDDEN NATIONAL EVENTS, it is highly unlikely that the denizens of Ambridge who almost to a man failed to notice the death of Princess Diana, would suddenly leave the village to take an expensive day trip to Greenwich.

MO TRAVIS A delightful lady who, while NEIL's JAILBIRD of a wife was doing her time, took a shine to Neil and tried to get a look at his weaners. Being as wet as he is, Neil refused to go the distance, and when Jailbird came out there was a big scene after which Mo DISAPPEARED. This is most unrealistic, and we waited in vain to find a simmering rabbit in the Carter kitchen. Mo is a local woman whose children go to the same school as the Carters'. So where is she? Why does no one ever bump in to her?

MOBILE PHONE (HANDBAG HEBDEN'S) One of the unsung icons of Ambridge. Hebden's mobile phone heroically distracted him while he was driving so that he missed seeing ROGER TRAVERS-MACY heading for him and drove into a tree and a horse. Anarchists celebrated long into the night, and had the mobile phone been present, it wouldn't have had to buy a battery all evening.

MOBILE PHONE (JAAARN'S) Very useful because it enabled him to give a number for sultry SHARON to use without having to identify his love nest with horrendous HAYLEY. The fact that it would ring at an inconvenient moment never seemed to have occurred to him, but then we all know it never seems to occur to anyone.

MOBILE PHONE (MRS HIGH AND MIGHTY'S) Was ubiquitous at the time of her fling with her former husband, ROGER TRAVERS-MACY but has never been heard since. Maybe she was shocked by Hebden's experience and cast it into the Am.

MONT BLANC, THE A top-class knocking shop outside the village. People go there for special occasions and, as with THE FEATHERS, invariably find it full of other people from Ambridge. Very expensive, you won't find yer Grundys, Tuggers or Carters there, although JAAARN went there for his last 'hurrah' before meeting his end. SHULA and THE VILLAGE BICYCLE go there when they can persuade some upper-class chinless wonder to take them and indeed BRIAN used to go there when he was having his notorious fling with The Bicycle. Since we know that most characters from the village go there rarely, at other times it must either be closed or perhaps choc-a-block with the silent conversations of people from Glebelands, Hollowtree Flats, and other nearby localities.

MOUNTAINEERING TEDDY A generous and thoughtful gift from HARDWORKING SIMON to DAMIEN. It was given after a weekend away when Simon had been giving HARRIET WILLIAMS a good old-fashioned seeing to but pretended to have been rock climbing. Mountaineering Teddy was referred to in loving tones until *that* SLAP but since then seems to have become an un-bear. Damien has mentioned wanting his teddy but recently it seems to have lost its 'mountaineering' epithet.

MRS BARRACLOUGH A delightful old lady who was murdered by DR DEATH in 1996. Locke tried to claim that she had died of cancer, but we all know that no one in Ambridge has ever died of cancer. Her death was widely mourned by a whole bunch of village establishment figures who had never hitherto been heard to utter her name, let alone talk to her. Typically, THAT FISHER WOMAN couldn't be bothered to visit her during her hour of need. She kept going on about, 'I must get round to see her.' But of course she was too busy practising witchcraft, whilst spouting PC nonsense, to have time for real vicarly business like visiting the sick.

MR BARRACLOUGH Devoted son of the above, who was devastated by her murder and fought an honourable battle to get DR DEATH struck off. Memorable scenes include the CRICKET Club dinner at GREY GABLES when Mr B accused Dr D of murder in full view of his fawning team mates. Death had to be restrained from hitting him. Yet it's to be noted that at no time did Mr Barraclough make any attempt to become physical himself. Dr Death made all kinds of smears against Mr Barraclough, suggesting that he didn't take much interest in his mother when she was actually alive. This is an allegation that could have been levelled at the whole of Ambridge, but poor Mr B was working a long way from the village and doubtless no one had bothered to inform him of his mother's plight. It is a source of great regret that we never hear of him nowadays. He should be a bar fly at THE BULL – a constant reminder to Dr Death of the travesty he has made of the Hypocratic Oath.

MRS HIGH AND MIGHTY Jennifer has tended to spend a lot of her life going around with a mattress on her back, albeit a fairly expensive mattress since she married BRIAN. Her first child ADAM was begat of a liaison with Paddy Redmond, a lowly farm hand at Brookfield. She then married and had DEBBIE by ROGER TRAVERS-MACY, a hero for his role in ridding us of that troublesome HANDBAG HEBDEN. Poor old Roger was soon given the heave-ho when she caught sight of Brian Aldridge's wad. Since then she has been a complete stuck-up cow.

She managed to have a dalliance with posh John TREGORRAN, and then another with the jolly Roger. The biggest laugh was when Mrs High and Mighty started making a play for Saint SEAN MYERSON only to be told he batted the other way. Jennifer is unquestionably Ambridge's biggest snob but she does at least have a soft spot for her children. Rather too soft a spot in retrospect as they are all completely dysfunctional. At one time she used to fancy herself as a writer and even had a column in the *Borchester Echo*. She rather seems to have forgotten about this.

MRS POTTER She seems to have had a walking frame since the age of 16 but shows no sign of giving up. Has not been known to speak but her walking frame has been heard to scrape. We imagine that the dreaded and castist Archers Anoraks invite the frame to their events so that they can hobnob with it.

MR PULLEN One of the little indulgences the Ambridge cosy establishment allows itself is to make snide remarks about this poor gentleman who has a weak bladder. Naturally he is never allowed to speak. There is never any talk about getting Mr Pullen treatment, albeit that his problem has been the topic of sneering for around 20 years, and he has never been permitted any other characteristics whatsoever. He is yet another leaking example of the complete failure of DR DEATH to maintain a proper level of healthcare in the village.

MR SNOWY Before he became a philanderer, NIGEL PARGETTER was a strange androgynous Hooray Henry who used to scrape a living in an ice-cream van of this name. This dates back to the days when *The Archers* was in large part a slapstick routine. But don't knock it – the Mr Snowy ice-cream brought joy to the hearts of millions.

n

NASTY GINGER CAT To all normal-thinking people, everything about SHULA raises the hackles. So it came as no surprise when her characteristically pampered puss Tibby was attacked by what Shula pathetically dubbed 'that nasty ginger cat'. Fearlessly the ginger cat fought, emitting an audible snarl, the likes of which you would only expect to hear on the Masai Mara. Only the intervention of village wimp – the former ice-cream toting NIGEL prevented Ginger from having a go at DAMIEN. Ginger's day will come.

NATIONAL LOTTERY The launch of the Lottery was one of the few SUDDEN NATIONAL EVENTS which didn't go entirely unnoticed in Ambridge. The problem was that it was launched at a time when the PC view was that it was a cynical way of taking money from morons and giving it to artistic fat cats. Hence the only village folk to play it were the Grundys – in fact both FAT CLARRIE and EDDIE played it without telling each other because they were both so ashamed of what they were doing. No one else in Ambridge played it then nor apparently has since, and it is now never mentioned despite having become an integral part of NHS funding and a right-on feature of Cool Britannia. Whether there is a Lottery terminal at the village shop has never been revealed.

NEIL CARTER It is difficult for Anarchists to like Neil, but we do try. He is an incredibly boring plodder who allowed himself to be bullied by his dreadful wife JAILBIRD into taking the most unsuitable job that he could possibly have taken – that of a sales rep. For ages we were treated to the harrowing scenes of him trying apologetically to sell feed nuts to all the Ambridge farming folk. It was quite clear that Neil was not up to this work and it seemed to be on the cards that he would lose his job and the F-reg. Datsun Sunny that no doubt accompanied it. Yet, amazingly, he kept the job for yonks and we never heard of the trials and tribulations of sales from one year to the next. He seemed to have become the John Harvey-Jones of Ambridge. When Neil eventually ended his employment with BORCHESTER FEED MILLS it was a great surprise that he walked out on them rather than the other way around.

Since he came to the village, Neil has wandered around with a justifiable inferiority complex that has never noticeably improved. Before he married Jailbird he tried his hand, or other parts of his anatomy, with a number of the village ladies, most of whom were way above his social standing and gave him the elbow. He was engaged to a bird called Julie who was a real Brummie townie, but that one never got off the starting blocks. Interestingly Neil is another of the village's many convicted criminals, as he was done for possession of drugs some years ago.

A most pathetic sight for many years was Neil being led on by SHULA. It's not surprising that she was later to come a cropper with HARDWORKING SIMON, because she has always been such a tease. Poor Neil would have given anything to go the distance with her, but she always ended up giving him the brush off. Neil's finest hour was while his Jailbird wife was doing porridge, and he almost had a fling with MO TRAVIS. 'Almost' is about as far as you can ever imagine Neil going when it comes to rumpy pumpy, in fact one has to presume that EMMA and Christopher are down to the AID man.

To his credit, Neil finally stood up to Jailbird and confessed his undying love for pigs. Since HAYLEY JORDAN has undergone a highly unlikely conversion on the road to the pig sty, it would be rather nice if Neil gave Jailbird the trotter and shacked up with

Hayley instead. The pair of them could walk happily ever after in a porcine wonderland.

NELSON GABRIEL Only someone of the most CASTIST disposition would seek to suggest that Nelson should be 'killed off'. However his behaviour in disappearing from the face of the Ambridge earth is bizarre in the extreme. As a former robber and architect of the great Ambridge mail van robbery (a crime for which he was tried and wrongly acquitted) there was a great irony when he began flitting from one Costa del Crime to another. It is understandable that Nelson became weary of the endless procession of middle-class bores who trooped through his wine bar. And it has always been something of a mystery how he ever acquired even the slightest knowledge of antiques, so no surprises when his antique shop was sold off.

The strangest thing about Nelson is that he has a posh voice despite being the progeny of one of the village's carrot-crunching bumpkins. Presumably educated at local rural schools, merely being a criminal does not seem a sufficient explanation for his refined pronunciation.

Nelson's sexuality has always been the subject of great speculation, though we all remember his black silk sheets and the attempted seduction of Jackie Woodstock. He has a daughter who is, ironically, a copper, but in latter years Nelson has come over as Borchester's Quentin Crisp.

His eponymous wine bar has never seemed to be a great success as it was always a place where middle-class yuppie Ambridge types like SHULA, ELIZABETH and NIGEL would go when they needed to talk quietly and earnestly (no doubt spinning out a half bottle of Frascati for four hours). Places where you can always get a table are useful but not much of a recommendation unless you are talking of MFI.

Following Nelson's disappearance in 1998, Elizabeth

announced in a dramatic and tearful voice that she had received a phone call from him and we would 'never see him again'. This was somewhat odd given that nowhere on earth is more than a few hours on a long-haul flight.

NIGEL PARGETTER A prime example of what can happen when an expensive education is lavished on someone who, in former times, would have walked about the village with a pig's bladder on a stick. Nigel is an upper-class twit who has always wanted to get inside SHULA's knickers and probably has done. In fact at one time he used to call her 'Shuli' – a term of affection that had any self-respecting Anarchists running for the safety of the LAVATORY.

Like many in the village he is a convicted criminal, having been charged jointly with Shula of the serious offence of 'taking and driving away'. He married 'Lizzie' as very much a second-best and because she shared his educationally subnormal slapstick sense of humour. In recent years we have felt a little more sympathy with him especially because ELIZABETH has been playing away with HORNY HUGH.

With saintly Shula back on the market, it is surprising he has not tried to get her back on side, though he probably recognizes that with her horse-hair blouse goes a complementary pair of iron knickers. For one delicious moment (during the Horny Hugh episode) the nation held its breath when Nigel appeared to be about to go the distance with THE VILLAGE BICYCLE. He presumably fancied her wonga as well as a bit of single wicket, and on her part he was ... well ... someone else in trousers. That it came to nought was a national disgrace.

O

OAK APPLE DAY Another of the complete failures as a theme night to try and revive the ailing fortunes of THE BULL. It was attended by the Snells, and that was it. It was a typical example of the total bankruptcy of imagination where the Perkses are concerned. Who was likely to get excited by Oak Apple Day when you can go to a drag night at THE CAT?

ONE-EYED MONSTER, THE Mike Tucker (or Tugger as he calls himself) is one of life's losers and an unreconstructed sexist. As a result of an industrial accident he has had only one eye for some years, but we very rarely hear any reference to this. Not exactly New Labour, he was at one time the trade union rep at Brookfield. He has enough chips on his shoulder to start a McDonalds restaurant, which is typical of the kind of hare-brained scheme he would come up with.

It is always surprising that anyone is prepared to enter into any entrepreneurial deal with him since nothing he turns his hand to is destined for success – for example, the STRAWBERRY CROP. He is permanently in a state of simmering anger and is very much in the category of people who call their lunch 'dinner'. But of course, as with everyone else, you'll never hear a genuinely bad word pass his lips.

1 + 1 = 3 It is rarely possible for two people in Ambridge to have a conversation without a third person joining in. This seems to happen particularly when they are discussing something of a confidential nature. Sure as night follows day someone will bound up to them and barge into the conversation with not the slightest degree of sensitivity.

ORGAN FUND Any charity fundraiser will tell you that if you set up an appeal, it is important to structure it properly, to report how much it has raised and to what extent the goal can now be achieved. The Organ Fund at St Stephen's was set up several years ago now, long before the days of TFW who would probably rather see the organ replaced with guitars and a steel band. A number of busybodies got involved in raising funds and at least one event took place. We've never heard another word about what happened or where the money went. But you probably don't have to look much further than who were the churchwardens at the time. One was FAT MAN FORREST.

ORGANIC VEGETABLES Boring though they are, they deserve a mention as they are grown by PAT and TONY. One of the many right-on things to occur in Ambridge is the existence of their organic crops. Considering the rip-off price these things are in our supermarkets it is hard to understand why Tony and Pat go on so often about being hard up.

OVERENTHUSIASM This was the euphemism which was used in court to describe HARDWORKING SIMON's behaviour which had allegedly resulted in DEBBIE ALDRIDGE receiving some minor bruising. She claimed it was actually the result of a RIDING ACCIDENT but as she is a pathological liar it is best not to believe her.

OVER-60'S CLUB Does it still exist? It can't be the most rockin' and rollin' of clubs since its events seem to be highly sporadic. The annual coach trip happens about as regularly as a total eclipse of the sun. Of course one of the things that doubtless hampers its success is the sheer volume of silent people who attend any of its functions. It must be most dispiriting for a guest speaker.

PARISH COUNCIL It is strange that whilst VILLAGE PRO-DUCTIONS occupy an absurdly disproportionate amount of time we hear virtually nothing of the Parish Council for months, sometimes years on end. Yet the Council must meet several times a year and will have numerous subcommittees. It is also rather odd that an old dipso like GEORGE (ALCOPOP) BARFORD has been allowed to continue as its Chairman for so long. We could really do with a list of all the members because there don't seem to be many people actually on it.

PAT ARCHER If we were to sum up Pat in a few words it would be an economic Uncle Tom (not Forrest we hasten to add). She has always been one of the village Lefties and has tended to make life hell for the more conservative and down to earth TONY, who she has been worn down by years of constant nagging. The discovery of the joys of capitalism has largely silenced her political ramblings and she is Ambridge's yogurt queen, ruling the dairy with a rod of iron. Pat's succession of inevitably low-paid female staff are bullied and generally treated like something the cat brought in – ironic given that her product is something the cat would like to take out.

The role of Pat and Tony is to be always on the cusp of success but never quite achieve it. They are carefully positioned to contrast with BRIAN and MRS HIGH AND MIGHTY who are always one step away from obscene wealth and THE ONE-EYED MONSTER whose fingernails are the only things standing between him and the abyss.

Pat is never far away when there is a death caused by a farming-related vehicle in the offing. She was in the car with

POLL DOLL when Kevin's MILK TANKER slammed into them, and of course JAAARN's death by THE FERGIE was another bummer for her. Pat has coped with the death quite well and has been relatively unfazed even by LANCASTRIAN TOMMY's assertion that she had effectively nagged Jaaarn to death. Whilst he did not exactly choose the most sensitive time to offer this opinion, it is not without some foundation in truth. However, if we can be permitted one enormous CASTIST indiscretion, we could point out that she has come a long way since being Jimmy Clitheroe's sister.

PEEEP ARCHER One recurrent theme is the naming of children within the Archer clan. The name is never determined by what is or is not a nice name. Instead it is used as a mechanism to curry favour (for example, the late JAAARN was named John Daniel in order to get a mention in the late DAN's will). So Peeep is actually named after PHIL. After all, you never know when there might be a Brookfield partnership up for grabs do you?

Like all the children of the cosy establishment, Peeep is a precocious little brat. Surprisingly, by the taciturn standards of Ambridge folk, she is speaking already. One of her first utterances bodes ill for the future: 'There's Stephen. I don't like Stephen.' It won't be long before Stephen finds he's taken a dive into a slurry pit, mark our words.

Peeep threw a bit of a wobbly when her brother BSE Josh was born. The usual sort of sibling jealousy, but of course it had to be dealt with in a very PC way. Poor old DAYVEED had to take a day off work to parade Josh in front of Peeep's class at school. Much to the chagrin of us all, Josh proceeded to 'fill his nappy' on prime-time suppertime radio. Miraculously, this one visit removed all traces of jealousy.

Peeep was unfortunately disfigured for life at the village fête a couple of years ago. Horrible HAYLEY applied a toxic face paint to her – just what you expect from someone who spends their life looking after children.

PEGGOI WOOLLEY Owner of SAMMY the cat and wife of JECK, Peggoi can be a bit of a pain. Where *did* she get her rather posh voice? She is another of the characters whose voice bears no relation to her parentage. Mrs Perkins, her mother, was a cockney with a voice to match. Peggoi is worth a copper or two having at one time owned THE BULL, and lives a life of luxury at GREY GABLES.

Peggoi is treated very much as a milk cow by her grandchildren and seems to enjoy dispensing largesse – always with strings attached. The best thing about Peggoi is that she doesn't approve of THAT FISHER WOMAN, since she has no truck with vicarettes. She has stuck to her guns and now worships at All Saints, Borchester, a good Bentley's drive away. Peggoi is also fairly lukewarm about THE VILLAGE BICYCLE ever since she tried to lure BRIAN away from Peggoi's awful daughter.

Peggoi clearly sees herself as Ambridge's conscience and who are we to argue? She is something of a prude and is always more likely to be heard saying, 'I don't think that's very nice' than '***kin 'ell, let's go down the pub and get slaughtered.'

She's a bit of a busybody and tends to go in for a lot of 'third-party sulks' almost always relating to her children or grandchildren. Invariably the way these work is that someone hasn't told her something, she's come to hear of it, and is now known to be upset about hearing it *and* the fact that she wasn't told.

PERIODS More or less half the population of the world have periods, but in a sedate place like Ambridge we do not need to hear about them. In recent years, the falling standards we have come to expect have reached the village and there are now two or three occasions when periods have raised their heads.

BRENDA TUGGER and EMMA CARTER started having them (note that it only happens to the common people), much to BEDDY's surprise and concern, and Kate stopped having them. Anarchists tend to be a bit squeamish about these sort of things, especially when we are about to have our evening meal at 7.00p.m. Strangely, but much to our relief, we hear much less about MEN'S PROBLEMS.

PHALLUSTAIR BLANDVOICE The current vet is only one of a long string of vets to put it about with the better-heeled womenfolk in the village. Over the years, the dreaded SHULA and THE VILLAGE BICYCLE have ensnared more vets between them than MR PULLEN has made trips to the LAVATORY. But Phallustair really takes the biscuit when it comes to charisma bypasses. He actually manages to make the late HANDBAG HEBDEN seem a bit of a player. Unfortunately he is just the kind of cosy character that the Archer clan love.

It would be nice to know a bit more about the first Mrs Blandvoice, as Anarchists still cling to desperate hopes that he might yet turn out to be a serial killer. Phallustair, as he is affectionately known amongst Anarchists, obviously came on the scene with just one aim – to get goalside of the St Michael label in Shula's sensible knickers. It is quite possible that by the time you are reading this, Shula, DAMIEN and Phallustair will all be shacked up together at Glebe as one nauseatingly cosy family. Phallustair has done much to ingratiate himself with Damien and was heard to tell him a very disturbing and inappropriate story about a polar bear who had a mouse for a friend. Hardly the stuff to fill the head of an already possessed child.

Phallustair is ridiculously unrufflable and, as with many other people in the village, he managed to appear without arriving. Perhaps he could DISAPPEAR without leaving – another beloved trick of many loved and hated characters.

PHIL ARCHER Although he is clearly a real stalwart of the village, and now in his 70s, it is difficult for Anarchists to know what to make of the blighter. Phil is very much part of the cosy establishment but he is also pretty boring. It is hard to think of anything he has ever done or said that gets the pulses racing. His judgement over the years has been pretty good. He seems happy enough being married to a FOGHORN, and it wasn't his fault that he married someone so combustible before that.

Phil manages to get up the nose of his equally boring son DAYVEED and has been unnecessarily tolerant of the daughter-in-law-from-hell ROOOTH who, ever since arriving as a student, has managed to grab his son *and* a partnership in the farm. Unlike Foghorn, Phil has the measure of ELIZABETH and KENTON and recognizes them to some extent for what they are. He has always been lukewarm about NIGEL, who he has long recognized as the dickhead we all know him to be. But where Phil has a ludicrously soft spot is for the dreaded sanctimonious Shula. As someone who has always been cautious with his money, it was rather surprising that Phil was so ready to bail out his waster of a son Kenton when it transpired he owed an unspecified sum to the Aussie revenue.

A couple of years ago Phil entered some kind of crisis which resulted in him spontaneously becoming a cooking maniac. This was very serious since not only did it get in the way of his running of the farm, but it caused friction with the Foghorn for whom cooking is her *raison d'être*. At its height he would insist on cooking Christmas dinner, and was to be found with his head permanently buried in Delia Smith, so to speak. Happily, he seems to have forgotten his new-found hobby completely, and is barely likely to switch a kettle on, let alone cook a meal.

As the patriarch of the Archer dynasty, Phil does not expect to be crossed and there was a wonderful moment early in 1998 when the Foghorn sided with Roooth and Dayveed over the perennially mind-numbingly boring question of whether or not to expand the herd. Poor old Phil was cut to the quick by the fact that even his beloved Foghorn had veered from her automatic pilot. Sensible Phil will doubtless pootle on into senility, at which time he will, like his father before him, be dragged kicking and screaming from Brookfield, finally surrendering to Dayveed and the Geordie gorgon.

PIANO The piano plays quite an active role in the village. THE DOG WOMAN, PHIL, and possibly ELIZABETH play it, and EDDIE was once sick in the one in THE BULL. No wonder SID and KATHY's restaurants never take off.

PC Many Anarchists get rather uptight about the amount of political correctness that creeps into Ambridge. The examples are too numerous to mention in much detail and of course proponents of the new PC world will often argue that it doesn't go far enough. The arrival of USHA brought a whole bundle of inappropriate Ambridge situations to our attention. When she arrived, PEGGOI was rather anti – but the notion that some upper-middle-class woman would get excited over the arrival of a high-caste, well-heeled Asian solicitor was most unlikely. On the other hand, the full-hearted welcome accorded to her by all the other inhabitants of this unfriendly, bitchy village is equally hard to swallow. Similarly, when Usha was suddenly subjected to terrorist attacks from a couple of Nazis who didn't live anywhere near the village, this had a ring of untruth about it. The celebration of DIWALI in Ambridge was of course the most natural thing in the world.

Other forms of political correctness surround people such as KATHY PERKS with her great desire to pursue her own career, and the portrayal of poor SID as a chauvinist husband. The real issue there is not KATHY's right to a career but the fact that Sid only bought their share of THE BULL on the basis of Kathy's former enthusiasm for and commitment to running a restaurant, and her loss of interest threatened the viability of the whole enterprise. That debate will rage on. Ambridge is, in truth, the quintessential PC village.

POLITICS There is very little mention of party politics in Ambridge, although the political leanings of a few have been quite obvious at various stages. HANDBAG HEBDEN was an SDP Councillor, SHULA, NIGEL and Tim Beecham were all members of the Young Conservatives in their day. FOGHORN was anti-grammar school, which didn't stop her sending Shula to Borchester Grammar, and PAT and THE ONE-EYED MONSTER have made various socialist statements. On the other side, JECK and BRIAN have been known to make the occasional political comment, but by and large you just have to work it out.

POLL DOLL Polly Perks was a nice normal woman of a kind sadly lacking in Ambridge nowadays. She was everything that the dreadful KATHY is not in that she was pleasant, friendly and an excellent landlady for THE BULL. If she had but one fault it was that she was friendly with PAT, a crime for which she was to pay with her life when she was tragically squashed by a MILK TANKER. SID loved Poll Doll and has never properly recovered. Had she lived, you can rest assured that the vulgar excrescence that is THE CAT would never have been able to challenge the Bull as the focal point of the village.

POSTMAN There isn't one and hasn't been for years. NELSON almost murdered one when he committed the great Ambridge mail van robbery and Harry Booker delivered post for a while. God knows how they get their post nowadays. Since they spend all their time shouting and calling in on each other they

---

probably never bother to write anything. There is very little evidence that they ever communicate with the outside world, so perhaps there's no need for one.

PRODUCT PLACEMENT This is not a phenomenon confined to television. Indeed on radio it is in a certain way even more glaring when it does occur. For whilst you can casually leave a box of Kellogg's cornflakes on a table in a television production, you actually have to mention it on the radio. It manifests itself on *The Archers* in a number of different forms. The out and out reference to a brand name is relatively rare, although the manufacturers of WD-40 were no doubt delighted when DAYVEED suggested to someone that 'a spot of WD' might help shift a rusty bolt on a gate. Delia Smith got a good airing by Phil in his cookery spasm. *The Teletubbies* have been given a merciless plug with DAMIEN and PEEEP both suitably enthralled by this moronic pap. Vodaphone were given a nice plug when MRS HIGH AND MIGHTY was heard trying to contact the mobile of Morwena the wicked witch. What is more common is the placement of information advertising such as JAAARN crashing his tractor without a safety cab. The final manifestation is the promotion of certain events over and above the level that would naturally occur within that community – the most notable example being GAY PRIDE.

PRU FORREST It is many years now since FAT MAN FORREST read *Jane Eyre* and began to see Mr Rochester as a kind of role model. He then packed his wife Pru off to THE LAURELS where she has maniacally produced jams and other preserves from the comfort of her padded cell. Pru is in fact only in her late 70s and the official reason for incarcerating her in Stalug Luft Laurel since she was 70 is that she had a couple of strokes. It is far more likely that her moaning murderer of a husband preferred wandering round the village saying 'I miss moi Pru' to the task of looking after her.

It is easy to tell how long someone has been listening to *The Archers*, simply by the fact that if they claim that Pru has never spoken, you know they are relative newcomers. For at one time Pru was possessed of a rather ridiculous bleating voice, and would call her husband 'Taarm' rather in the same way that SHARON RICHARDS called the late John 'JAARN'. They had a couple of foster sons – Peter and Johnny – who are just another two of Ambridge's many DISAPPEARED. Given Tom's track record, their continued absence is particularly sinister. Perhaps, for once in their lives, the village cosies should remove the blinkers from their eyes and investigate the oft-dug gardens of the Forrests.

QUEENIE For a misogynist like ZEBEDEE TRING, naming a cat Queenie must have been an act of great self sacrifice. There is a long-established tendency for animals to be neglected in Ambridge and no one knows what happened to Queenie when Zebedee croaked it. But then what happened to Charlie when NELSON disappeared?

QUIZ Perhaps one of the reasons why THE BULL has become so unpopular is because of SID's propensity to start some enter-tainment feature and then discontinue it without comment. In the latter part of 1997 there seemed to be a quiz team that competed regularly and with some success against the silent teams of other pubs in Borsetshire. But this seemed to stop without a word of explanation. When he came up with the whacky and sexist idea of running a women's quiz team during the 1998 World Cup, no one was heard to ask what had happened to the regular quiz nights with the existing team of BERT, USHA etc.

RELIGION No one could accuse Ambridge folk of being a bunch of Bible bashers. And when you put your mind to it you suddenly realize that there is something quite sinister about the way religion is treated in this weird place. Appropriately enough most of the residents exist in a kind of Amish community with very little discernible contact with the outside world. There is, of course, St Stephen's but this is clearly a front for all kinds of pagan goings on and it is obvious that THAT FISHER WOMAN is a complete imposter.

Few of the residents ever refer to going to church apart from one or two of the token sanctimonious characters such as the awful SHULA and her cosy parents. Yet whenever we hear a service in Ambridge it sounds like a state occasion in Westminster Abbey, with hymns being belted out like nobody's business. On those occasions it is noticeable that FOGHORN is always completely ignoring the service and talking to someone in a huge stage whisper.

One of the strange things about Ambridge is the complete absence of Catholicism – the Reformation was obviously a pretty thorough job in Ambridge. JOE GRUNDY claims to be a Methodist but this would seem to be nothing more than a convenient excuse to avoid St Stephen's. We never hear that he's 'off down the chapel', and indeed whenever he quotes the Bible, which he is prone to do now and then in times of trouble, it is always the fire-and-brimstone passages – hardly the stuff of Methodism.

RIDING ACCIDENT Second only to that SLAP in its deliciousness was the occasion when the simpering DEBBIE

ALDRIDGE came a cropper at the hands of HARDWORKING SIMON. It is one of those occasions when we have to be honest as witnesses and say we didn't see a thing. All we know is that there was a lot of shouting on the part of both Debbie and Simon after which Debbie was allegedly a touch black and blue. She immediately attributed her state to having fallen from her long-suffering horse, Tolly, on the riding course. And who are we to doubt her?

Under pressure from THE VILLAGE BICYCLE and SHULA, both of whom carried a long-term vendetta against poor Simon, Debbie changed her story and Simon was landed in court. Debbie is clearly unstable and has had numerous unsatisfactory relation-ships with men. It is almost certain that she was hallucinating, and that Hardworking Simon was just being gallant in carrying the can. The manful way in which he pleaded guilty in order to save Debbie from having to testify in court never received the praise and admiration it deserved. What a shame this misunderstood man is no longer in the village to add his own colour – black with a tinge of blue.

ROBERT SNELL A somewhat sinister figure whose life is entirely consumed by computers and CRICKET. Robert calls his good lady 'Lindybottom', but sadly we rarely get to hear this. He is somewhat lacking in charisma and has been rather unkindly stereotyped as a computer nerd, when of course we all know that no more than 95 per cent of computer buffs can truly be described as such. Robert had a job 'in computers' which no one seemed to know about in any detail, and then it all went pear-shaped (what *is* wrong with the shape of a pear?). This meant that Lindybottom had to get on her bike and look for menial tasks to help earn the family crust.

Robert is on his second wife, having bored the first one into submission. The most exciting thing he has ever done since his arrival in Ambridge is to almost move to Grimsby – a career move scuppered by Lindybottom's efforts to assist him.

ROBIN STOKES A very boring vicar-vet who had two children called 'Salmon Oliver'. He had two characteristics of note. The first was a weird speaking voice that sounded like Noël Coward singing 'Mad Dogs and Englishmen'. The other was that he suffered from one of the MEN'S PROBLEMS: impotence. He was all set to marry THE VILLAGE BICYCLE but after HANDBAG HEBDEN had tried to mow her down in his kamikaze attack, she suddenly realized that Stokes hadn't got a big enough wad. Robin could hardly be described as 'over the moon' when the Bicycle not only broke off their engagement but rapidly married poor old loaded GUY. Robin moved away in abject misery, although he probably got the last laugh when he realized how close he had come to being bumped off, for the marriage to Guy only really lasted long enough for him to change his will.

ROGER TRAVERS-MACY He is one of the heroes of *The Archers*. By trying to imitate David Coulthard along the narrow Ambridge lanes, Roger managed to rid us of the least interesting character ever to grace the airwaves – HANDBAG HEBDEN. He wasn't going to be put off by a few horses clogging up the highways, and it certainly wasn't his fault that Handbag was on his MOBILE PHONE at the time.

Roger picked MRS HIGH AND MIGHTY out of the gutter when she was a single mum and married her. But his struggling antiquarian book business couldn't keep the spoilt woman in the style to which she wished to become accustomed. We all thought he had disappeared from the scene until one day he showed up at Home Farm and whisked Jennifer off her feet once again. Poor old BRIAN, a man whose morals are above question and whose old-fashioned standards of decency are a credit to him, was understandably mortified. Travers-Macy by now seemed rolling in it, presumably as he has now gone in to the far more lucrative hard-porn business. He gave the awful DEBBIE a flash car – a totally inappropriate gift for a girl that goes round in sackcloth and ashes most of the time. Sadly Roger the dodger seems to have disappeared again.

ROOOTH ARCHER The whinging Geordie has assaulted our ears for several years, ever since she arrived at Brookfield from Harper Adams Agricultural College as a student on work experience. She managed to inveigle her way into Brookfield, marry DAYVEED and is now a partner in the firm. Roooth has produced two sprogs – PEEEP and BSE Josh, the latter sired by BSE ANDY. It is notable that she spends as little time as possible with her children. She is forever palming them off on the FOGHORN to look after and it has been suggested that she may well be suffering from Munchausen's syndrome by proxy.

Roooth, like Debbie, is paranoid about being ignored in decision making. This is ironic as she tends to sulk her way into getting exactly what she wants. There is no question that she prefers the company of cattle to children – whenever a relief milker is needed, this inevitably creates a far greater hoo ha than finding a babysitter. The poor milker is then harangued by Roooth, which must be galling to experienced cowmen.

ROY TUGGER Roy has long been the working-class member of the brat pack and for some time was seemingly welded to the bar of THE CAT. As the son of THE ONE-EYED MONSTER, it is inevitable that he will carry traces of spud on his shoulder. Yet for a complete dumb cluck he has had some quite interesting moments. While at his FE college he fell in with two gentlemen named SPANNER and CRAVEN who held strong views on the subject of immigration. In a trice, Roy went from one of the 'silent' to fully fledged Nazi, something for which he seems to have been entirely forgiven. Whilst no Anarchist could condone their behaviour, there can be few who would not have wanted to post a turd through USHA GUPTA's front door if only in the hope that DR DEATH might slip on it.

The extremely unlikely coupling of the dreary Tugger boy with KATE ALDRIDGE was never going to be an easy one. The young Tugger does not appear to have any particular interests or ambitions but is increasingly sensible – always a bad sign.

The murder of his friend JAAARN did raise a number of interesting issues. Tugger had been threatened by Jaaarn just a few weeks prior to his death when Jaaarn told him that if he ever touched 'his HAYLEY' he'd 'kill' him. Though he never got the chance, was it just because Tugger took preventative action? After all, young Roy was already making great strides towards bedding Hayley on the old rebound.

Ted Hughes began to shake in his shoes when Tugger popped up at Jaaarn's funeral with a somewhat finger-down-the-throat poem he claimed to have written himself. Strangely, this poem was reprinted in the *Radio Times* shortly after, when it was said to have been written by someone else. Is the lad actually living in a Walter Mitty world, and is this bit of plagiarism another sign of the built-in inadequacy of the Tugger family? Bookmakers, of whom there are none in Borsetshire, will give odds on whether or not he will marry Hayley or return to Kate as father figure to her Caribbean baby.

S

SAMMY PEGGOI WOOLLEY's long-suffering puss who once drove Peggoi to say the memorable words, 'No more pilchards until I get a decent miaow out of you.' It has generally done the normal cat-like things such as getting lost or locked in places, being a bit ill, etc. Has been known to speak somewhat more than TRUDY PORTER.

SAMMY WHIPPLE This man is quite simply a saint. Saddled with a ridiculous Hardyesque name, Sammy worked in the feudal environs of Home Farm where he had successive indignities heaped upon him. If Sammy wasn't being patronized by MRS HIGH AND MIGHTY, or lambasted by BRIAN, he was suffering the humiliation of having daffy DEBBIE bossing him around. Sammy suffered the final insult in 1998 when he was made redundant with the minimum possible redundancy of £6000. To add insult to injury, DR DEATH, who, remember, was shacked up with Sammy's solicitor, repeatedly made malign smears as to his tendency to swing the lead over his poor health. They don't make shepherds like that anymore and the Aldridges didn't deserve him. Perhaps in his retirement he will decide to take up speech as a hobby. He might find that he enjoys it.

SEAN MYERSON Sean is our very first declared homosexualist. For years, we have wondered about the sexual proclivities of various characters but Sean actually 'came out' without even a by-your-leave and shouted his sexual preferences from the rooftops. MRS HIGH AND MIGHTY had the hots for him and was clearly disappointed but she doesn't give up, and is always keen to have long drawn-out discussions with him on interior decorating. She quite clearly hopes that he will reveal himself to be more of a bi-guy.

Like any minority in Ambridge, Sean is almost entirely without sin and it falls to Anarchists like ourselves to uncover the vile character behind the pink exterior. We now know him to be a collaborator in Benefits fraud since he was allowing KATE to work for him when he knew she was claiming dole. Sean is clearly on a mission to see THE BULL closed down so it is hardly surprising that SID is not his number-one fan. Indeed, Sean's first act on taking over THE CAT was to steal an outside bar concession from Sid. Like a number of characters, Sean did not 'arrive', he was just suddenly 'there'. No one knows where he or his partner Peter came from, and we are sure there is a lot more to emerge in due course.

SEX The permissive society has been slow to reach Ambridge. Scenes of rampant sex and debauchery are few and far between, but that does not mean they do not exist. Long-term listeners will know that SHULA has been deflowered more times than a Christmas cactus, and well we remember a sordid scene in which she was rogered by journalist Simon Parker in a cornfield. But, in the main, sex is alluded to in the most coy terms – there is occasional talk of 'early nights' amongst the establishment figures. ROOOTH and DAYVEED turned up to Christmas lunch with hay in their hair, and the likes of HAYLEY and SHARON make lude sexual innuendo from time to time. But Anarchists believe that within the village there lurks beneath the surface every kind of sexual perversion known to man, woman, and (without a doubt) beast. We are given such a goody-two-shoes version of life there, that it has become obvious that we are being duped.

SHANE Until early 1998, a prominent member of the non-speaking fraternity. Shane was a member of the ever-growing homosexualist mafia that seems to have taken a grip on Borsetshire's catering industry. His only job was as chef at NELSON's wine bar. All one ever heard of him related to tantrums and prima donna-ish behaviour, but then he did have to endure the burden of working for old queen Gabriel. He was unceremoniously made redundant when the wine bar was shut down amid a welter of CASTISM surrounding the reasons for Nelson's disappearance. He will soon be forgotten as we reflect sadly that he who lives by the quiche shall die by the quiche.

SHARON RICHARDS We have always been somewhat mystified about how GEORGE (ALCOPOP) BARFORD in his role as Parish Councillor managed to get SHARON fixed up with a COUNCIL HOUSE. Housing is not a PARISH COUNCIL responsibility – this would fall in the jurisdiction of the District Council relevant to that part of Borsetshire. On the other hand, there has only ever been one Councillor in living memory in the village who served on anything other than the Parish Council, and that was the late HANDBAG HEBDEN. Anyway, presumably in return for sexual favours, boring George swung it so that Sharon was able to move from her caravan at Bridge Farm.

Sharon, poor girl, has been dealt one of life's sorry hands. She has always had good taste in men, and got together with young CLIVE HORROBIN to produce the delightful and ever-silent KYLIE. She lived with Gerry Buckle, one of Ambridge's vicars in the good old pre-THAT FISHER WOMAN days. Whether he was giving her one was never made clear, but there's no such thing as a free vicarage is there?

The snobby socialist PAT ARCHER always detested Sharon, partly because she used to drop cigarette ash in the yogurt when she worked for her in the dairy, but more so because she didn't think her good enough for her JAAARN. A talented hairdresser, poor Sharon only needed a break. She loved Jaaarn and, for a while, they lived a life of bliss in the council house. Eventually pressure from the Archer mafia forced her to move to Leeds, breaking Jaaarn's heart in the process. When she returned, she soon saw off the shallow HAYLEY, who was little more than a Brummie voice and a bunch of sexist attitudes. Sharon's womanly charms were just what Jaaarn needed, and who didn't sympathize with the lovely couple when horrible Hayley caught them at it? The true un-Christian nature of the Archer community, That Fisher Woman, *et al.*, really came into its own when Jaaarn died and they deliberately didn't make the effort to let Sharon know. She missed the funeral but at least came back to let Hayley have it with both barrels afterwards. Chances are we will see little of her as there is nothing left to attract her to Ambridge. But it would be rather nice if she came back to give LANCASTRIAN TOMMY a quick introduction to the *Kama Sutra*.

SHIFFON GUPTA USHA's brother is a refreshingly genuine character. He hates white people and sees his sister as a bit of an Auntie Tom. He can't understand what she sees in DR DEATH, but then he hasn't seen his trusty sword. Very much 'new man', Shiffon was disgusted by the fact that Dr Death tended to leave all his clothes lying around and expect Usha to clear up and do the housework. Sadly he seems to have softened towards the doc since he got so involved in the great DIWALI celebrations a couple of years ago.

SHIRES The name of the local brewery, and unique in that it only sells the one eponymous beer. No 'special', 'best', or 'winter warmer' – you have a pint of Shires or lump it. Sold in THE BULL, but probably not at THE CAT. You might have thought that the brewery would have some employees and that once in 47 years someone in Ambridge might have worked there, or an employee moved into the village – not a bit of it.

SHULA HEBDEN (MURDERESS) In fact, cosy establishment figure Shula Hebden, universally loathed by Anarchists, is at least a *double* murderess. To start with it was very convenient that she should be the one, and the only one, to 'find' DORIS dead, given that she was coincidentally the heiress to Glebe Cottage. We all know that she gave her a helping hand, just the odd cushion, Brookside style. She was probably dormant for several years until she cunningly managed to call husband HANDBAG HEBDEN on his MOBILE PHONE to do a spot of nagging, just as he was trying to negotiate a winding lane full of cars and horses. We strongly suspect that she was involved with THE VILLAGE BICYCLE in the murder of GUY but have never been able to prove it. Shula was the acknowledged village bicycle before Caroline came on the scene and it is ironic that they should be such good friends, helping to create the village tandem.

We are often asked why we dislike Shula with such vehemence and the reason is that she embodies the sanctimony and goody-two-shoes smugness of the Ambridge establishment. She is a dreadful do-gooder and has a veneer of a complete absence of malice. She has frequently been nominated by Anarchists as the person we would most like to see immersed in a vat of boiling oil. In addition to her successful career as a murderess, for which she remains unconvicted, she does have a conviction for 'taking and driving away' which does not make her the ideal choice for a churchwarden.

Her attitude to HARDWORKING SIMON was highly hypocritical. Remember that the Shula who took exception to Simon's dalliance with HARRIET WILLIAMS was the same Shula who has led men such as NEIL CARTER a merry dance and has had more blokes than GEORGE (ALCOPOP) BARFORD has had hangovers. Shula no longer needs to work, having made a packet out of the insurance wonga from her late husband Handbag. As Estate manager, working for Rodway and Watson, she milked the business and ran the office like a social centre. Any time anyone wanted free photocopies they only had to turn up. Shula was frequently compromised by the fact that members of her family were tenants of the Estate. Justice was done in the end as her career ended with her instant dismissal for gross misconduct in testifying in favour of the layabout Grundys against her own employer at the tribunal. The notion of declaring an interest never seems at any stage to have occurred to her. Shula has become increasingly self-indulgent and self-centred in recent times. The extent to which she gradually sought to seduce DR DEATH and her appalling treatment of PHALLUSTAIR is quite shocking. The future for Shula is probably one of cosy and stomach-churning bliss until DAMIEN begins to sink his fangs into his cousins. Mind you, we would always be very interested in seeing the exhumation of Doris.

SID PERKS Yet another criminal, for a long while Sid was not even legally entitled to hold the licence of a pub. Over the years he has, on the face of it, eschewed his criminal ways and become the mainstay of THE BULL. And what a job he has there. He nowadays suffers from huge competition from the local gay bar, THE CAT AND FIDDLE, where naturally most of the village folk prefer to drink. Possibly this is a reaction to the hare-brained theme nights he has put on to try to attract the punters. If The Bull is to be a success then KATHY has got to go. You simply can't have a pub where the landlady harbours a pathological hatred of customers, cooking and serving behind the bar. His best bet would be to do a runner and go down under to join his daughter. But we would be devastated to lose Sid. His strangulated chicken noise when he gets angry would be irreplaceable.

SIGNATURE TUNE Interfering busybodies at the BBC who feel compelled to change everything have occasionally tampered with our signature tune. The daily version is a reworking of a previous version, but the most outrageous interference was to substitute the normal orchestration for the ridiculous accordion-dominated row that now greets us on a Sunday. The accordion is not a musical instrument but a hand-operated kazoo, and Anarchists have never accepted the Sunday signature tune. It is a memorial to meddling. The revered signature tune has been used to great dramatic effect in the past although nowadays they don't seem bothered to use it so. For example, a dramatic ending would usually be given a part of the tune starting Da Da Da Da Diddle idlle Da, Da Da Da Da Diddle idlle Da, Da Da Da Da Diddle idlle Da, etc. before then going into the usual tum te tum te tum te tum. Sad isn't it?

SINGLE WICKET TROPHY Despite the fact that most people were only too glad to forget the awful HANDBAG HEBDEN when he rather cruelly drove into a horse and killed himself, SHULA insisted on donating a trophy to his memory. This is an irritating habit widely practised in amateur sport and culture and results in a proliferation of pieces of meaningless silverware, turning AGMs into interminably boring events. They also result in acrimonious infighting, associating the dear departed with an annual commemorative fist fight.

There are in fact two trophies bearing this name because when the late JAAARN won it he had the good sense to file it in a drawer out of sight. He forgot where he had put it and was forced to have a replica made. Happily they have different inscriptions. One says 'to a very dear friend', the other says 'to a true and trusted friend' though the trust did not seem to extend to him not running you over when he was on the phone – if you were a horse.

A regular winner of this trophy was of course Jaaarn Archer, whose untimely squashing by a tractor will doubtless mean that, by the time you are reading this, some misguided do-gooder will have landed the unfortunate Ambridge CRICKET Club with a tacky memorial tractor.

SLAP The most glorious moment in two decades was when HARDWORKING SIMON allegedly slapped SHULA. It was widely agreed that she deserved it for years of sanctimony and cosiness. Indeed even the generally left-of-centre journalist LIBBY PURVES famously wrote that, 'Someone had to slap Shula'. Anarchists however take the view that Simon, one of nature's gentlemen, merely took the blame for Shula hitting him. We all heard a slap but none of us saw it (a bit like the RIDING ACCIDENT). Readers of the Anarchist newsletter actually voted by a large majority that what in fact had happened was that MOUNTAINEERING TEDDY had fallen from the mantlepiece, upsetting a bowl of cold custard which had fallen face down on a stone floor. You'll just have to make your own mind up. Whatever the cause of this small noise, Shula didn't half make a fuss about it, went into purdah for about two weeks, until she blabbed to THE VILLAGE BICYCLE who of course did her best to escalate the situation. In typical churchwardenly fashion, Shula sought to blackmail Simon by saying she'd publicize the slap if he tried to sack the idle JAILBIRD CARTER from the Estate office. Now there's professionalism for you.

SMOKING AND DRUGS These play a disappointingly small role in Ambridge PC life. KATE was heard to exclaim 'I'm dying for a fag' once. She has also been one of few people to introduce the wonders of dope to the village, although it was brought in by her then housemate JOLYON GIBSON. So successful was she in this that her parents spent a very cheerful evening with her and enjoyed a particularly elevating soup. Of course if BRIAN lived up to his reputation as a disciplinarian he should have been tough on crime and marched her to the police in true Jack Straw fashion.

The other person to have brought dope into the village was NEIL CARTER, via a girlfriend many years ago. The only mentions we ever really hear of smoking are highly judgmental comments from parents when children have been caught smoking behind the bike sheds or, since not many people in Ambridge have bikes apart from WIWYERM GRUNDY and LYNDA SNELL, over at LAKEY HILL. There have just got to be some magic mushrooms on LAKEY HILL or over in MARNEYS. The lovely SHARON RICHARDS enjoyed the odd ciggie or 50, and there has been mention of GEORGE (ALCOPOP) BARFORD and his pipe. But Ambridge awaits its first heroin junkie with eager anticipation.

SPANNER This was one of the gentleman colleagues of ROY TUGGER who decided to persecute USHA on the basis that she was completely unreal and lived with the appalling DR DEATH. Because he went a bit too far in putting a turd through her letter box and giving her a free sample of his ammonia fragrance. He was thrown into jail along with his good mate CRAVEN. So far as we are aware they are both still on Death Row. Whereas CLIVE, who was imprisoned for a spot of armed robbery, was quickly out and about again, these two have never surfaced to date.

STRAWBERRY CROP Increasingly dull in its annual re-appearance is the joint venture between THE ONE-EYED MONSTER and NEIL to grow strawberries and run it as a pick-your-own. Since both Neil and The One-eyed Monster operate with an inverted Midas touch, there is always a different plague to hit it. In 1997 it was destroyed by rain, and what wasn't destroyed was eaten by KATE's alternative friends. During the Nazi period of Ambridge, SPANNER and CRAVEN mistook it for Donnington Race Track. The other problem is that there never seems to be anyone available to man the shop so most of the strawberries just walk.

SUDDEN NATIONAL EVENTS Ambridge folk are always caught out by events in the world outside their village. They either ignore them completely or one person in the village makes a brief allusion to it and that is the end of the matter. When Princess Diana was killed, there were a hasty mention, a weird monologue from FOGHORN in St Stephen's (where she didn't actually mention it), and that was it – no books of condolence or special events. On the day of the funeral, life in the village carried on as if it had never happened.

Few national disasters are mentioned in Ambridge, and there is never any question of anyone in the village having been involved. The explanation for all of this is probably that, as far as we can tell, most of the villagers never set foot outside the place, and would therefore be unaware of what was going on. No one listens to the radio or watches television and we never hear anyone mention a newspaper other than the *Borchester Echo* which is probably produced somewhere in the village using a John Bull printing outfit.

SWEARING However angry they get, and they do get very angry, people in Ambridge hardly ever swear. The 'F' word is unheard of and those who would be most likely to swear – the late JAAARN, DAYVEED, ROY and NEIL – never resort to bad language. Strangely it is the women who are most likely to conjure up the odd expletive when pushed to the brink. THE VILLAGE BICYCLE has taken solace in foul language on at least two notable occasions, each a respectable few years apart. On the occasion that JECK WOOLLEY shot the lynx she said, 'Why did you bloody do that?' She also described her stepson, the much-maligned HARDWORKING SIMON, as a 'shit'. DEBBIE called the self-same Simon a 'bastard' during his bout of OVER-ENTHUSIASM. She also said 'bugger' when the phone wouldn't work at the time of the post office visit by CLIVE. An aural pinpointing has it that THE ONE-EYED MONSTER called some-one a 'bastard' on 27 March 1983. Eddie has managed a respect-able 'bloody' from time to time. Apart from that – sweet FA.

J

TAIL-BITING One of the many nasty animal-related problems suffered by farmers but only mentioned once in a blue moon. *The Archers* was originally designed in part as a farming information programme, so one cannot help but feel sorry for any farmer who tuned in to the first episode in the hope that he might find a cure for tail-biting in pigs. But all he needed was a bit of patience for, sure enough, some 46 years later he will have heard his answer. Anyone could have told him: house the pigs on a bed of straw.

TAMAGOTCHI Ambridge never fails to surprise us with the aspects of modern life that it ignores and those it takes to its bosom. ROBERT SNELL, a serious computer person, was one of the first people in the country to obtain one of these children's toys. LYNDA, ever ready for a child substitute, was only too delighted to look after it when Robert was away. Since it is a pocket-sized object it is rather surprising that Robert felt it necessary to leave it in her care rather than take it with him. In retrospect it was a particularly bad decision on his part, as she killed it.

THAT FISHER WOMAN TFW has become one of the Anarchists' most detested characters. She embodies virtually everything we hate – political correctness, superficial 'niceness', a characterless voice, and the fact that she was immediately welcomed by the establishment within the village. Her contribution to the spiritual well-being of Ambridge folk has been nil. She has brought a load of delinquents to the vicarage for a holiday, had the half-baked idea of producing a 'peace quilt' and otherwise peddled right-on claptrap amongst a grateful conservative audience.

TFW has a completely indeterminable sexuality and we just don't know if her preference is men, women or sheep. The one thing we know it isn't is bats, as she has done her best to rid the church of this endangered and protected species. When her arrival in the village was first mooted, a ridiculously small number of people objected, but the only one who held out was good old PEGGOI WOOLLEY who has now taken her hassock elsewhere.

Whenever she has the opportunity to do something vicarly, she flunks it. She couldn't be bothered to go round and see poor MRS BARRACLOUGH when she was being helped on her way by DR DEATH, which in some ways makes her an accomplice in the whole sordid business. When JAAARN ARCHER was murdered it was yonks before she turned up at Bridge Farm to offer comfort to poor PAT and TONY. We'd like to see someone get up to a bit of single wicket with her – the sooner the better.

TITCOMBE The gardener at LOWER LOXLEY, and probably the character with the silliest name in Borsetshire though no one ever laughs at it. He's not helped by having no Christian name, but then Morse seemed to manage OK. Titcombe was treated like dirt by JOAN but is now patronized by the dreaded NIGEL and ELIZABETH. You might have thought the days when young upstarts could call a loyal employee by his surname are long since gone, but then perhaps it's his Christian name.

TOKEN OLD FARMING RETAINERS Seasoned listeners will know that there is always an old yokel who works at Brookfield, is given special dispensation to speak and must always have the same voice. Anarchists cannot necessarily remember the first ones but take for example Ned Larkin who popped his clogs back in 1967. There was no mention of him dying, he was simply replaced seamlessly by his son Jethro who had exactly the same voice, and eventually we heard occasional allusions such as

THE ARCHERS ARE REAL – THERE IS NO CAST!

'Remember poor old Ned'. At least, thanks to DAYVEED, we knew when Jethro shuffled off this mortal coil. He was replaced eventually by BERT FRY who, though only in middle age, had the same old decrepit voice that is standard issue for his role. There are numerous silent farming retainers who are suddenly invented and in many cases never alluded to again. They make excellent workers – they never go in the pub or the shop, never gossip, just simply toil.

TOMMY CROKER QUARTET, THE JECK WOOLLEY's favourite function band for events at GREY GABLES. They are a cross between Motorhead and The Dead Kennedys – a fine bunch of musicians. We never actually hear them and this makes them the ideal band for those occasions when you don't want to shout to make yourself heard.

TONY ARCHER You can always recognize Tony by the substantial chip on his shoulder. Although it falls somewhat short of the giant spud that adorns the epaulettes of THE ONE-EYED MONSTER, Tony has always had a problem about not being his rich sisters. Being married to Ms PAT ARCHER who inflicts the double whammy of being both a feminist and Welsh is a cross he has had to bear for some time, and Anarchists tend to find his 'call a spade a spade' mentality quite refreshing for the most part. He's a hard-working chap, although it is written in his tea leaves that a good 50 per cent of anything he touches will turn into the proverbial brown stuff. In his heyday Tony was quite a stud and it is very disappointing that he has been so reluctant to put it about since he got married to Pat. It's such a pity he didn't marry the fragrant Mary Weston to whom he was once engaged, life might have been so much kinder to him. His decision to go organic was rather PC but quite ahead of its time.

Since the death of JAAARN, Tony has become rather dull. He

has a growing and alarming tendency to be nice to people and to get less agitated about things. He seems to have acquired the philosophy that once your son has been squashed by a tractor it doesn't really matter if someone wants to put a pipeline through your farm. Whilst in some respects this is an understandable position it could lead to a worrying increase in tractor sales to property developers.

TRACY HORROBIN It is very sad that we never hear a peep out of young Tracy. By all accounts she is everything that her awful social-climbing JAILBIRD of a sister is not – fun, a live wire, attractive, in fact a really nice girl. Naturally Jailbird rarely mentions her, but she is a real credit to her hardworking mum Ivy and Anarchists would like her to be given her rightful place in village life. One option is for NEIL and her to strike up a relationship. It is very noticeable that Tracy never pops round to Jailbird's, presumably because she wouldn't be welcome – too much of a prole. We say, give her a chance.

TRAFFIC NOISE Traffic in Ambridge works on the tree falling in the forest principle. Every now and again, someone (usually LYNDA) becomes concerned about traffic in the village. When this happens we hear a constant sound of heavy lorries and cars being driven too fast as a background to every outdoor scene. Indeed we could be forgiven for assuming that Ambridge is in fact an M5 service station. Yet as soon as the campaigner tires of the subject we are back to the peace and tranquillity that we all love. No one seems to realize that the best riposte when one of the village busybodies starts up a petition about heavy lorries or whatever is simply to suggest they forget about it and it will go away.

TREE BRANCH The murder weapon used by DAYVEED

ARCHER to kill the TOKEN OLD FARMING RETAINER Jethro. It is only because members of the Archer family seem to enjoy an immunity from prosecution usually reserved for foreign diplomats that he has never been brought to book.

TREGORRANS, THE There's no real class in Ambridge nowadays. It's mainly new money. John and Carol TREGORRAN and their privately educated daughter Anne were dead posh, kind to the riffraff, benevolent and superior. They sort of fizzled out without any explanation. They belonged to the era of Lawson-Hopes, Brigadier Winstanley and Ralph Bellamy. They had a maid called Nancy – there are no known maids or housekeepers in Ambridge now (with the possible exception of Mrs Brown who, if THE VILLAGE BICYCLE hasn't murdered her, used to look after the late GUY PEMBERTON and was presumably inherited along with the Dower House).

Carol had her own market garden and vineyard. The village aristocracy would regularly get pie-eyed on Manor Court wine. When the Tregorrans were spirited away, Manor Court and the vineyard must have gone with them because they have never been mentioned since. Oh, those were the days!

TRUDY PORTER For many years, Trudy's only claim to fame was the elevation of her chest: flat. She is one of those characters who has been around so long that she must be well into her 40s by now. Yet whenever she is mentioned, it is as if she is no more than a flighty teenager. Trudy has worked at GREY GABLES for over 20 years and has always been referred to in a somewhat sneering and dismissive way. Just because she doesn't want to talk. But who would want to talk if the only people to talk to were JECK, LYNDA, THE VILLAGE BICYCLE, JEAN-PAUL or HIGGS?

When a junior management position was created at Grey

Gables to replace the awful KATHY PERKS, who was departing to have her sprog, Trudy finally came into her own. As with any job selection in *The Archers*, the applicants are invariably people we've heard of and so the choice was between the educated and enthusiastic Lynda Snell and the silent Trudy. Poor old Lynda never had a chance because she gets up The Bicycle's nose, so Trudy got the job and has never been heard of again. Indeed, if we did not know better we might believe that 'someone' has forgotten that Trudy got the job, since Lynda always seems to be standing in when The Bicycle is away.

TWINNING Ambridge has been twinned with Meyruelle since September 1994. Meyruelle is the setting for 'an everyday story of garlic-eating, beret-wearing lamb burners'. As with many Ambridge activities there is never any continuity with their twinning. You can go years without any excursions taking place or even a fleeting reference to it. Then it will suddenly dominate life for three months – it is almost volcanic in its behaviour. When the village gets 'twinning fever', FAT CLARRIE starts trying to turn her pot noodles into exotic French dishes and SID remembers that he is actually running boules tournaments on an ongoing basis. There have, of course, been visits each way, though it would appear that the majority of those residents from Meyruelle who come over to Ambridge are Trappist monks.

U

UNDERWOODS Borchester's department store, it is always full of people from Ambridge and no one else. People like MRS HIGH AND MIGHTY seem to live there, and it appears that there is nothing which cannot be found in the place. Underwoods is always spoken of in respectful tones and one gets the impression it is the Harrods of Borsetshire. This is rather strange since it is obviously one of the dwindling number of independent stores and such places tend to be redolent of Grace Brothers rather than Harrods. No one ever visits a supermarket, and why should they when they can go to Underwoods Food Hall and stuff themselves with PAT's overpriced yogurt? In fact there are only three retail outlets ever referred to in *The Archers* – Underwoods, 'the cash and carry' and the village shop.

USHA GUPTA Anarchists have a bit of a problem with Usha. She consistently tops the poll along with SHULA as the character most of us love to hate, The fact is that Usha is a token figure who has slotted herself into the life of the village with an almost seamless ease – well that's PC for you. This is hardly surprising because Ambridge is one of the most liberal-minded communities on earth. No one has ever made a racist remark, and even the old folk of the village who have never set foot outside the place in their lives are only too happy to welcome Usha as if she was a sister. The cosy establishment in the village have really gone over the top in their desire to toady to her – particularly noticeable when Usha was invited on to the Playground Committee when there would have been many more obvious candidates.

It was all something of a mystery when she suddenly became the victim of horrendous racial attacks. Here she was in the middle of a rural village where she was universally loved, and suddenly she was getting turds through the post – hardly surprising then that the village doesn't have a POSTMAN any more.

Usha may be a top-notch lawyer, but a cook she ain't. As far as we can tell both she and DR DEATH are completely incapable of even boiling an egg. They will regularly drive to Borchester to obtain take-aways, or otherwise they will eat out. This is somewhat strange since vegetarians are invariably good cooks, if for no other reason than to save themselves the problems of having to endure the unimaginative attempts of the carnivorous majority to produce vegetarian fare.

Usha Gupta has remarkably few relations. Apart from her brother, we only ever hear of Auntie Satia. Presumably her relatives are staying away out of disapproval that she is shacked up with Dr Death. Usha's days are numbered: it is only a matter of time before she is MRS BARRACLOUGHed, and the good doctor now has his designs firmly fixed on Shula anyway.

V

VEGETARIANISM There have been plenty of vegetarians in Ambridge over the years. Virtually every young woman in the village: ELIZABETH, KATE, and LUCY have at least dallied with it long enough for us to be given endless lectures on the cruelties of meat production. USHA is one but that's all to do with her religious beliefs.

VILLAGE BICYCLE, THE Caroline Bone arrived in the village as a cook at THE BULL. The establishment tend to regard her with affection, but the truth is that she is a calculating self-centred manipulator who has been laid more times than an Axminster carpet. She thought nothing of deserting poor old SID to work in competition to him at GREY GABLES, and how ironic that she would eventually inflict the final humiliation on her erstwhile employer by becoming a part owner in the ailing Bull.

Caroline's finest hour was when she seduced BRIAN ALDRIDGE, much to the distress of MRS HIGH AND MIGHTY. But as a rule you will find that she has had a sexual relationship with any remotely professional person who ever shows his face (or any other part of him) in Ambridge. In most cases she leaves behind a broken heart but she has certainly done well financially. When her Uncle, Lord Netherbourne, pops his clogs, she will probably cop a whole load more dosh.

Caroline's conquests also include vicar-vet ROBIN STOKES, Dr Matthew Thorogood, and former Estate owner CAMERON FRASER. In fact Cameron was stolen from her by the equally scheming ELIZABETH, but Caroline was undaunted. As soon as Fraser did a John Stonehouse, she had her claws into the new owner, the loveable old buffer GUY PEMBERTON.

Here we saw Caroline at her most cunning. She hatched an evil plan – to marry poor old Guy and then drive him to an early grave. Caroline was well aware that the ghastly SHULA had the hots for HARDWORKING SIMON and was fearful that if that relationship should continue she could be kissing goodbye to serious wonga. She duly married Guy and then proceeded to make his life a misery by endlessly telling him unsubstantiated tales about Simon's relationship with HARRIET WILLIAMS. Eventually Guy could take it no more, his heart gave out, and The Bicycle inherited the Dower House and half THE BULL. Not bad for a few months' work.

Poor Guy was hardly cold in his grave when The Bicycle's mind turned to whom she could seduce next. Unfortunately she had exhausted every middle-class or above male in the village. She advertised in the lonely hearts section of *Borchester Life* (one of those publications which had never been mentioned before or since). Inevitably, of all the millions of people she could have met, she managed to talk to someone and actually arrange to meet him without realizing until she got there that it was someone she knew: the LOONY LARRY LOVELL. After that experience she played hard to get with GRAHAM RYDER who obviously was simply not up to her bank balance. You don't need to be Mystic Meg to see that her next target will be PHALLUSTAIR.

VILLAGE POND So far as we are aware the pond is completely full of vomit left over from the GCSE celebration party organized by LANCASTRIAN TOMMY in August 1996.

VILLAGE PRODUCTIONS Urgh, urgh, urgh, argh ... Every year we have a tedious pantomime or Christmas show, and nowadays we often have a summer one as well. The storyline is *always* the bloody same. LYNDA *always* wants to direct it, others *always* try to wrest control from her, but they *always* fail. No one, except BERT FRY and the Grundys, actually wants to be in it. No one wants to attend rehearsals and we always have endless scenes with people pretending to act – quite ironic really, particularly when someone like BORING CHRISTINE gets involved. The people who the director most wants in the production *never* want to be in it. And the people who do end up in it are permutations of the same narrow bunch of village cosies.

The most awful thing about village productions is that we have to listen to weeks of rehearsals culminating in the performance itself which usually occupies the whole of an evening slot. What we hate about these productions is not so much the fact that they are repetitive, cosy and dull, but that there are millions of other things that must go on in the village at the same time that we simply never hear about. We accept that it might be odd suddenly to dispense with these shows, but the fact that we don't hear every tedious description of the proceedings does not mean they are not happening.

W

WALTER GABRIEL Even non-*Archers* devotees know the name of Walter Gabriel. But it is a wonder that, when Ambridge has been populated with people like that, we have ever survived to the 1990s. Walter was a ridiculous, incredible character who wheezed and giggled in a manic way and whose sole contribution to village life was to say 'Me old pal, me old beauty' *ad nauseum*. Walter had a monotonous tendency to inflict his woodcarvings on small children.

WEATHER This is a very important subject in a farming community. The success or failure of crops can depend on it, yet it is mentioned surprisingly rarely in Ambridge. One possible reason for this could be that when they do start to discuss their weather it is sometimes completely different from that experienced by the rest of us. Once, the harvest was interrupted by torrential storms at a time when the whole of Britain was caught in the middle of a drought.

As recently as Christmas 1997, farm vehicles in Ambridge were falling foul of black ice and people were bemoaning the cold weather while the rest of England enjoyed the mildest Christmas in living memory.

'WHAT ARE *YOU* DOING HERE?' This and other slightly less aggressive derivations such as 'What brings you here?' or 'What can I do for you?' are stock phrases which are trotted out with unbelievable regularity. In a small village where people are constantly going to encounter each other, this rather 'in-yer-face' confrontation seems quite unnecessary, yet amazingly no one ever seems to mind being asked. Never do we hear a 'mind your own business'. The enquiry is always greeted with a courteous explanation to justify one's presence on earth.

WIWYERM GRUNDY Young master Grundy looks set to carry forward the torch of poaching and deceit borne with such pride by his family over the years. On the rare occasions when he speaks, Wiwyerm shows an unhealthy interest in animals and anyone who wants to go round with GEORGE (ALCOPOP) BARFORD must have ulterior motives. We suspect it was Wiwyerm smoking behind the cow sheds that caused the Grange Farm fire which resulted in thousands of pounds worth of damage and a very hot dog.

One has to be sorry for the lad when he has his mother growling 'Wiwyerm' at him every few minutes, though admittedly this happens somewhat less frequently nowadays. By dint of a cunning bit of Grundy flattery, THE VILLAGE BICYCLE took on the role of Wiwyerm's godmother. This was an excellent piece of business that has more than paid for itself already.

X The letter X is the bane of any self-respecting A–Z compiler's life. Even the *London A–Z* baulks at an X. Sadly, Ambridge is no different. You might expect that during the course of 47 years someone would have launched a successful career as a xylophonist, but of course the residents of Ambridge are largely philistines and the percentage of musicians has always been negligible. Nevertheless, if we may be permitted the most naff and vulgar distortion of the English language imaginable, we will here discuss the ...

XTRA EPISODE 1998 saw one of the greatest cons in the history of mankind. We were told that we were to get an extra episode on Sunday nights. The fact is that this is constructed entirely out of the minutes casually lopped off each weekday episode. The result is we are being expected to listen more often but are not getting anything extra.